M000085362

Athletic Sc...
Step By Step Blueprint For Playing College Sports

Lynn West

Copyright Athletic Scholarship Info © 2013

Published by Lanie Dills Publishing

Chapter 1
Recruiting - It's Up To You

Image Credit Photoxpress

College bound athlete! One of the most exciting times of your life will be when you are playing high school sports while simultaneously trying to secure a college athletic scholarship.

Your hopes and dreams of playing your sport in college are now within view. All those practice sessions, training camps and high school games are about to pay off.

The experience is truly exciting and exhilarating for you, your friends, and your parents. You may even begin to feel that you definitely will be recruited and will be awarded the athletic scholarship of your dreams. The reality is that you do not have the scholarship until you sign the Letter of Intent.

So, no matter how much ballyhoo is going on, keep that in mind. This is not the time to leave this very important process to chance. Keep your wits about you until you actually sign with a school. Remember the college coaches are selling their programs to athletes at this time.

Several of them may be calling you everyday and it would be easy to begin to feel that you could let up some on your own recruiting activities.

There are countless stories of good athletes who went through this whirlwind of recruiting activity only to fall through the cracks. Don't let this happen to you.

Enjoy this exciting time, but be aware that it can also be one of the most frustrating, confusing, and overwhelming times of your life. This manual is intended to inform you, the student-athlete, and your family about the recruiting process or the **"game"** of pursuing an athletic scholarship.

To be successful, you must take control of this process and you must learn how to maximize your chances of obtaining the athletic scholarship you are seeking.

This up-to-date guide can give you the confidence, information, and the tools you will need to place yourself in contention for your much-desired athletic scholarship. Experts agree that the most prized commodity in the recruiting game is "information". College coaches and prospective college athletes both succeed or fail by information or the lack of information.

Athletes need to know where they can receive a scholarship and how to go about getting one; college coaches need to know about athletes who will best benefit their programs.

Years ago, most college programs spent a minimum amount of time and effort on recruiting. The recruiting process mostly consisted of scouting the local high schools and relying on high school coaches to send along information about promising athletes.

Today, the recruiting process is highly sophisticated; and, in most cases, demands that student/athletes know how to market themselves. Many well-intentioned coaches, parents, and high school guidance counselors, who are advising student-athletes today, do not understand the steps in the recruiting process.

Additionally, the vast majority of them were never college-recruited athletes themselves; so, they may be giving kids, hoping for a college athletic scholarship, incomplete, erroneous, and potentially damaging information.

Teaching you how to systematically develop and put your various marketing pieces into a winning package is just a part of the overall strategy taught in this guide.

We'll also show you how to put your marketing package, your unique information, in the hands of the college coaches. We'll show you how to gain their attention and how to keep their attention focused on you.

Obtaining your athletic scholarship is a process consisting of a series of steps. The more steps you complete, and the better you complete them, the more you increase your chances of obtaining an athletic scholarship.

As a student-athlete, you can help your chances of qualifying for an athletic scholarship by demonstrating superior athletic skills and by passing the required academic courses with a satisfactory GPA. Good timing and good luck may also come into play; but, undoubtedly, the most important thing that you can do is to learn how to promote yourself to college coaches.

There are some key reasons why a student-athlete is not recruited. Lack of talent, lack of the required GPA, and lack of coach exposure are all among them.

Talent doesn't necessarily mean that you must have been an all-state athlete. It does mean that you have probably obtained one or more of the following: all-conference, all-county, all-state, all-tournament, or one of the various Most Valuable Player honors; or, at the very least, you have been a starter for your team.

If you have goals, a plan, some talent, the required academics and GPA, heart, dedication, a good work ethic, and you're also willing to learn how to market yourself; your chances of receiving an athletic scholarship will be greatly increased.

The sooner a college coach knows about you, the better your chances are of getting a scholarship.

It will be your job to see that you are noticed early before all the scholarships are awarded. If you are a student-athlete who learns and uses the marketing techniques found in this guide, you will be dramatically ahead of your competition in getting your information to the college coaches.

If you are one of the rare "blue chip" athletes who comprise a very small percentage of the potential scholarship recipients, you will more than likely be recruited without having to contact the coaches yourself.

However, you will still need to know how to conduct yourself and what will be expected of you during the recruiting process.

You will also need to know how to keep yourself eligible. Academic problems are by far the most common way that student-athletes become ineligible.

There are, however, many less common circumstances, which could also cause you to become ineligible.

For example, you could accept money or other things from a prospective college coach or booster club. This would cause you to become ineligible under the current NCAA guidelines.

Remember, college athletics is big, big business involving billions of dollars. It is important to know that the activities of other people such as your high school coach could even cause you to become ineligible.

Recently, it was alleged that a high school coach was paid $200,000 to steer a "blue chip" student-athlete to a particular Division I school.

This type of scandal could cause the student-athlete to become ineligible to play for a college program and could also easily affect his or her entire potential professional career.

With this much at stake, isn't it worth knowing the rules and regulations governing the "game" of recruiting?

If you are not a "blue chip'" athlete, you will need all the information in this guide to effectively promote yourself to college recruiters and to maintain your eligibility status.

Accurate, up-to-the-minute information is the key to achieving your dream of playing college athletics. As I've said previously, it can be the most exciting time of your life, a wonderful time that you will never forget; but it can also be as puzzling as a rat maze. Crucial attributes you should have or be willing to acquire in order to accomplish your goal of obtaining an athletic scholarship:

1) It is **imperative** that you have some natural given talent. As I've already said, you don't have to be an absolute superstar, but you must have talent. Don't focus on just one sport unless, of course, you enjoy competing in only one sport.

An all-around athlete will usually be recruited over a player who happens to be good at just one sport. Whatever your sport, you must develop and continually practice those drills which will improve your overall conditioning, coordination, strength, and speed.

2) **You** must be fundamentally sound, no matter what your sport is. "Fundamentally sound", means you should be able to execute the basics of your sport flawlessly. For example: if you are a basketball player, there is no excuse for having a poor free throw percentage.

3) **Heart**, desire, the "never-quit-attitude" are all attributes that can't be taught, you either have these very valuable qualities or you don't. If you are offered and decide to accept an athletic scholarship, it should be your commitment to yourself and your team that you will always compete at your very highest-level right down to the very last split second. It shouldn't matter whether it is a practice session or a competition for a national championship.

4) **Believe** it or not, a good academic record can greatly increase or decrease the number of schools that might offer you an athletic scholarship. More on how this works later.

5) **Character** is living your life in a way that makes you proud of yourself. No matter who you are, your character could probably be improved.

College coaches will be hesitant to give an athletic scholarship to someone who has had problems in the past. They reason, if you have had problems before, you probably will again. All things being equal, coaches will usually shy away from the possible problem athlete who might bring negative attention and disgrace to their programs.

You should always give them good reasons to recruit you, and avoid anything that would give them a reason not to recruit you.

6) **You** must develop or already have an overall-winning plan. Your plan must include those steps, which will eventually get you noticed by college coaches. No matter how good you are, you won't get a scholarship if college coaches don't know about you. Again, you must have some talent to receive an athletic scholarship.

However, by following the advice given throughout this guide, you will better understand the recruiting process, which will enable you to better manage your efforts towards obtaining your scholarship.

Use this information to put your best foot forward during every step of the recruiting process. You may not be the top recruit; but, at least, you will have a good chance to be a recruit. The tools you will need are provided, but it will be up to you to pick up these tools and use them.

When it is all said and done, it will be important for you to know that you have exhausted every opportunity to maximize your chance for a scholarship.

Chapter 2
Evaluate Yourself

Your pursuit of a College Athletic Scholarship will be more effective and much easier if you can learn to look at yourself through the eyes of the college coaches. It may be difficult at first, but think of yourself as a commodity, a piece of the puzzle, a part of the plan, a potential asset or an investment.

You'll be more successful from the start if you will learn to view yourself in this way. You've probably never looked at yourself or even thought of looking at yourself like this.
It seems cold and calloused; however, you'll be way ahead in the **GAME** of college athletic recruiting if you will develop this approach.

Coaches are hired to produce winning teams. More to the point, college coaches are hired for their ability to bring in additional revenue to the school. Their jobs depend on their ability to bring success for the school.

For that reason, they are under relentless pressure to produce winning teams. They may be attractive, charming, and be able to handle a radio or T.V. interview, but if they don't recruit those athletes who make up winning teams, they won't stay long. College administrators and athletic directors recruit coaches and eventually select and hire the one who they think will be able to put together a WINNING TEAM.

The whole process is much like the one you will go through in your recruiting process. College athletics is an enormous business involving many, many billions of dollars. Winning teams draw attention (more loyal fans). Radio and T.V. want to feature winning teams and are willing to pay big bucks for the right to cover these games, (more viewers mean higher paying advertisers).

A company like Nike might pay a school several million dollars for the right to furnish the school's athletes with Nike gear. Why?

Because the more times Nike products are seen, the more products Nike sells, (more buyers). The focus on winning teams is important to you because you must learn to look at yourself as an investment.

When the coach offers you an athletic scholarship, he or she is expecting a return on the school's investment in you. The school is putting the money down up front in the form of your athletic scholarship expecting that you will be a part of an overall winning game plan. They are expecting you to be a profit maker, a MONEYMAKER. When you can picture yourself in this light, you will know how potential coaches will be evaluating you. You'll be looking at yourself through their eyes.

If the coach doesn't think you will produce a return on the school's investment, you won't be offered a scholarship. It's that plain and that simple.

Now that you know what's ultimately behind the college recruiting game, you can successfully create your own unique recruiting package which will be designed specifically to promote you as an athlete that will bring not just a good return but a terrific return on the school's investment in you.

First, realize that you will need to be in control of your recruiting game plan. Don't made the mistake of letting your high school coach, counselor, parents, booster club member, friend or any other person or company be in charge of it. This is not to say that you won't need the help of other people or that you can't utilize the services of specialty companies like resume, video editing or even recruiting companies.

However, just remember that you will always need to maintain your status as manager of your recruiting game plan whether you do it all yourself, have help, or hire part of it done. If you do decide to contract with a company to do all or part of your package, make sure that you have an agreement with them that you will be kept up-to-date with the progress at all times.

In fact, you should develop a system of tracking all activities. We've provided a sample-tracking sheet, which you might find useful for this purpose. Take responsibility from the start and you will be able to put together a winning package that will insure you of the best possible opportunity to be awarded the athletic scholarship you're seeking.

Since you'll be in charge, you will know what needs to be done and when. This **"take charge"** attitude will give you a tremendous advantage, and at the same time will reduce the level of anxiety and frustration.

You will actually being doing all the things necessary to get yourself recruited while most of your competition will be hanging around waiting for the phone to ring.

ASSESS YOURSELF

Are you a REAL High School Sports Recruit? Take a good, long, hard look at yourself keeping in mind the prospective college coach's point of view.
He or she will be evaluating you as a potential asset and will be looking at you as a potential part of a winning and money generating team. Put yourself under the microscope and size yourself up honestly. Consider your attributes, strengths, and weaknesses from every possible angle.

This exercise will most certainly be enlightening, but it will also give you a starting place for your recruiting game plan and will enable you to recognize and maximize your strengths. And, at the same time, you'll be able to see and either eliminate or minimize your weaknesses.

While completing this self-evaluation, compare yourself to other athletes in your school, your town, your state, your region, and nationally. Take out a piece of paper and write down the answers to the following questions:
1. Are you tall or short for your position?
2. Are you the right weight for your position?
3. How's your flexibility and balance?

4. How's your coordination (the way you move, balance, change direction, how your movements flow)?

5. How's your speed and jumping ability?

6. How's your strength (over-all strength, not just the bench press)?

7. Are you in tip-top condition, could it be improved?

8. How's your GPA? Are you willing to improve it?

9. What are your ACT & SAT scores? Can they be improved? You can take them several times.

10. Are you a troublemaker or do you work in harmony with the rest of the team?

11. Are you a hotshot ball hog or a dedicated team player?

12. Do you take advice from your high school coach? Constructive criticism? Note: Your high school coach is just one of the people who you should not "blow-off" during your high school career.

13. Do you willingly practice or do you have to be forced?

14. Do you work hard in practice or just slide by?

15. Are you weak in some areas and are you willing to put in the extra practice on these weak areas?

16. Do you play to win every minute of every game or do you play your very best just part of the time? Have you ever played your absolute best throughout an entire game.

17. If you consistently play in top form, how's your sportsmanship?

18. Are you excited about and do you enjoy playing your sport?

19. What's your emotional state and how will it affect your performance

20. Do you take drugs?

21. How's your speech?

22. Are you shy and introverted or outgoing and personable?

23. Do you know how to conduct yourself in public or would you be an embarrassment?

24. Do you have an "attitude"? Are you willing to adjust it?

25. Would you be willing to live away from home? How far away from home would you be willing to live?

26. How's your vision?

27. How do you rebound from injuries?

28. Have you been injured? Do you need rehab or surgery?

29. Why do you want to play college sports? For you or for your family?

30. Do you keep up with your studies on a daily basis?

31. Do you know how to study and prepare for exams?
32. Are you college academic material?
33. Are you a starter for your team?
34. Are your statistics impressive?
35. What kinds of recognition have you received in high school (all-league, all-county or state, etc.)?
36. What kind of local recognition have you had (newspapers, radio, TV)?
37. What were your evaluations like at any sports camps you attended?
38. Do you have the physical skills necessary to play at the college level?
39. Do you believe in yourself and in your ability to succeed in your sport?
40. How well do you rebound from disappointments and adversities?
41. Are you a leader or a follower?
42. Do you have heart?
43. Do you possess the winning attitude of a champion?

These are, of course, just a few of the questions you might ask, but I think you get the idea.

You want to establish where you are right now in every area. This self-examination will give you a base line, a starting point. Once you know where you are, then you can proceed to where you want to be. No one else will be seeing the answers to these questions, so be brutally honest. If you find that you're physically out of condition, what can you do to improve this negative?

Do you need to set aside more time for exercise, get a practice buddy, get a trainer, work harder, change your diet, or quit taking drugs? Whatever your weak areas are, find them and eliminate them or minimize them. Another example might be that you find that your size is smaller than the average athlete in your position.

Realizing that the scouts and recruiters will always be looking at the bigger, taller athletes first means that you will have to work harder to overcome these odds. Knowing this information at the beginning of your scholarship search will better prepare you to be successful.

You'll have to learn how to "out hustle" your competition. You'll need to make a commitment to excellence in your daily activities. When you know what your strengths are, you can build on them.

Even if you are the best in your school, your town, your city, or your state, etc., there is always room for improvement and there's always room at the top. As an example, for those sports requiring strength, college coaches will not automatically be impressed just because you can bench press more than anyone else in your state. College coaches are looking for strong players, not strong weight lifters. They want to see how explosive and powerful you are in the game situation.

Are you easily knocked off balance? Do you get run over and shoved around? Can you step up and charge your opponent? Show them that you can use your strength advantageously on the field or court. If you are not an "all star" player, finding and securing an athletic scholarship is basically a numbers game.

You will be sending 50-60 promotional packets. The idea is to be the best that you can possibly be so that your marketing package will stand out from the crowd. Avoid being discouraged, disappointed or demoralized if the top athletic programs do not recruit you. You will still have many opportunities to win a college education and to play college athletics. Compare your search for an athletic scholarship to a job search. You look for a job until you get one and you don't stop looking for a job after applying at just a few places. Have this same attitude with your scholarship search. Keep applying until you're successful.

Chapter 3
The College Sports Recruiting Process... What Really Happens

In order to obtain an athletic scholarship, you must certainly have talent; but you must also develop the ability to get the recruiters to notice your talent.

Chances are, you won't automatically be recruited just because you are a good player. While there are some 360 thousand NCAA student-athletes, there are millions of kids vying for athletic scholarships.

Recruiting has become more and more sophisticated and the competition has never been greater. In fact, some college coaches in some sports are now even recruiting internationally.

If you are not a sought-after "blue chip" player and you want to reach your goal of obtaining an athletic scholarship, then YOU will have to be instrumental in making things happen for yourself. Critical to making things happen, is your ability to get college coaches and or recruiters to know that you exist. Then, you must provide them the opportunity to see you play either in person or on video. If they don't know about you, they can't possibly recruit you no matter how perfect you might be for their programs.

Early in your Junior year, make a list of all the schools where you would be interested in playing. There are approximately 2000 schools, you need to make it your mission to gain and keep the attention of the recruiters and coaches at these schools.

Coach recognition is at least equally as important as having talent. If you are a go-getter this is great news for you because you can, to a great extent, be in control of whether you get a scholarship or not. The bottom line is, that in most cases, you will have to go looking for your scholarship; it usually won't come looking for you.

Knowing this at the outset will enable you to turn the tables on the recruiters. Locate the coaches and recruiters running those programs where you would be interested in playing and then you make the initial contact. The process of evaluating and selecting athletes is not an exact science. Recruiters and coaches find out about potential recruits in several different ways not the least of which is the prospect's own marketing effort.

Most recruiters spend more time scouting in highly populated areas because they can keep travel expense down and because they can see more prospects in a shorter period of time.

They can attend regional tournaments, for example, and see every potential recruit in the area in one trip. If you don't live and play in one of these areas, then you must redouble your efforts to get noticed.

Recruiters also sometimes visit schools that have a tradition of producing talented athletes to see if more promising athletes might be coming along.
Still other recruiters keep their ear to the ground to hear about talented athletes through the grapevine (other coaches, high school coaches, friends, and alumni). Major college programs have "spotters" or "scouts" that provide reports to coaches on prospective players subsequently recruiting him or her. However, keep in mind that the vast majority of schools operate with limited recruiting budgets. At these schools, your own marketing efforts will go a long way towards getting the coaches to notice you. In fact, you will be making their recruiting job much easier by promoting yourself to them.

Finding and securing the best talent for their programs is a big part of their jobs. By initiating the first contact, you put yourself in their recruiting system and you greatly reduce the time and energy they need to spend on searching for talent. Usually your efforts will be appreciated.

As we've already discussed in the previous chapter, college athletics is a multi-billion dollar business, therefore, the university tries to make sure when you are recruited that you will be a good investment This is where your self-evaluation can pay off. Ask yourself, what do I have to offer and can I help make the team a success? If your answer is yes, then take advantage of and create every opportunity you can to have your talents noticed by college athletic recruiters. More than likely, you won't have any idea that these scouts are observing you; however, they go to tournaments, camps, and AAU competitions for no other reason than to observe players and record information on prospective recruits.

It is extremely important that you compete at your highest level at all times. A scout may actually be at your game to watch one of your teammates or someone on the opposing team; but naturally, if you are playing well, you will be noticed too. **So play at your very best all the time.** Large Division I schools have large budgets to buy scouting reports, visit athletes, and offer campus visits. Their budgets provide enough money to evaluate many athletes. The coaches and scouts will travel long distances to watch a potential athlete play and to establish a relationship with a recruit.

MISTAKES TO AVOID
There are several mistakes you should avoid if you are to be successful in your search.
Below are a few ways that might kill your chances of receiving an athletic scholarship:
1). Waiting until your senior year in high school to start learning about the recruiting process. This delay could spell disaster. The more prepared you are in anything, the better off you will be; and there is no other area where this is more true than in the college recruiting arena.
Your grade point average, SAT/ACT scores, NCAA Eligibility Center, and your athletic skills are all areas that given enough time and effort can be improved upon. There are many resources available via the Internet to help improve your GPA and testing scores.
Be sure to also check out the admissions criteria for schools you are interested in attending. If you need assistance with admissions, check out the Admission Tips.

2). Depending solely on getting an athletic scholarship to pay for your college education. Seek out all possible avenues for other types of financial aid. Check for grants, academic scholarships, scholarships based on need, scholarships given by your community, church, companies where your parents work. Apply, apply, and still apply.

By obtaining other financial aid, you instantly make yourself more attractive to the athletic coach. The coach will be able to offer you a partial athletic scholarship requiring a smaller bite out of his recruiting budget.

Also, in spite of all your marketing efforts, you may not be recruited to play sports in college. You will want to have a back up plan.

3). <u>Waiting for a college coach to show interest in you.</u> This absolutely destroys many dreams of playing college athletics. Coaching staffs, in many cases, are overwhelmed with day-to-day duties.

Recruiting is very important; however, often coaches do just like a lot of the rest of us do. They do what is easiest and takes the least amount of time and energy which means that they recruit locally or in nearby cities.

If you are interested in a particular school, you should contact the coach yourself. Keep your name in his mind by sending a letter of introduction followed by additional information from time to time. Follow-up with phone calls to see if your information is being received. Don't make a pest out of yourself, but do let the coach know that you are really interested in playing for his or her particular program.

Your efforts will not only make his/her job easier, but it will also demonstrate your desire to play for that particular program.

4). <u>Waiting on your high school coach to contact college coaches for you.</u> There aren't that many high school coaches who have the necessary college contacts to help you. There are even fewer who have the time and energy to devote to helping you.

You should understand that if you are a better than average high school player, your high school coach needs to find your replacement as soon as possible. So, where will he be spending his time? In reality, his job is to expose younger kids to athletic programs, which will help them to develop better life skills as well as better athletic skills.

Of course, he also wants to have winning teams, but at the high school level, the emphasis is not so much on making money. At any rate, his main job is not to market you to potential colleges. Do not, in most cases, depend on your high school coach to obtain your college athletic scholarship for you.

Although some coaches will help, most just don't have the time, knowledge, or inclination to do so.

5) <u>Letting your academic life slide.</u> If you fail to keep your GPA up, you will be eliminating yourself from many recruiting programs. Among the first questions any college coach will ask about you is: What's your GPA? Turn your GPA into an asset and you will be in the very enviable position of having access to a full range of athletic scholarship opportunities.

Remember, the coach has only so much money in his budget for scholarships. The coach's job is to get the best and most talent with this limited budget.

If you can qualify for a partial academic scholarship then he can save money by offering you a partial athletic scholarship.

You will be giving yourself many more opportunities in college sports and in life by keeping your grades up. There are many, many resources available to help you shape up your academics. You must identify your areas of need and determine to improve those areas.

6) <u>Thinking that a letter, questionnaire, phone call, or visit from a prospective college coach or recruiter means that you are being recruited to play for that school and that you will be offered a scholarship.</u>

There are many steps to receiving an athletic scholarship. One of these initial contacts is just a first step.

Avoid thinking that you are home free at this beginning stage. When you started 1st grade, hopefully you were planning on eventually graduating from high school; but it was only the first step, and of course there were no guarantees. Receiving a letter or questionnaire from a coach or a prospective school should be considered in much the same way; it is just a beginning step. Thousands of these letters and questionnaires are sent to potential prospects each year. When you do receive one of these letters or questionnaires, see it for what it is; just that first step.

Fill it out neatly and completely, and send it back immediately. Coaches use these routine mailings as helpful tools to help them identify those student/athletes who might be interested in enrolling at their school. They are used to separating out those who are actually interested in their programs from those who are just checking things out (the tire kickers).

After you have responded to one of these letters, follow-up a few weeks later to ask if there is any other information you can provide. Any phone call from a coach or school can be considered another rung up the ladder toward reaching your scholarship goal.

A phone call means the coach does have some interest in you and wants to know more about you. You should still consider this first phone call just a preliminary contact. During the phone call, you should be very polite and try to give a great impression.
Be yourself, don't try to act older than you are, or say you understand something if you don't. This phone call would be a good opportunity to ask some questions about the program. Don't bombard them with questions, but asking a few will show that you are interested too. Try to say things that will keep their interest piqued. When, or if, a school requests a video, you should consider this request yet another good sign and another step up the ladder.

Make the video according to the instructions given in Chapter 7, or if you can afford it and want a more polished marketing piece, hire a video service to shoot a professional video. You can also check out the video service we recommend if you can't make one yourself.

Again, as with all requests from the coach or school, make sure you comply promptly. A visit from the head coach, assistant coaches, or an invitation for you to visit the school should be taken as a positive sign that things are headed in the right direction.
At this point you can be encouraged, but don't get the "big head"; you do not have the offer yet. It is very possible that the number of

potential recruits for your position has been narrowed down to two or three, but as of yet no decision has been made.

During the visit, appear neat, polite, interested, and eager to hear what they have to say and offer; however, don't appear that your life will end if they don't offer you a scholarship. When you visit the campus, watch to see how the coach interacts with his staff and the current players. Is this the way you want to be treated?

Also, talk with as many athletes as possible; not just the ones the coach asks to show you around campus. Ask if you can visit during a practice? This will give you some insight into how the coaching staff interacts with the team members.

If all goes well with this visit, you could soon be receiving your scholarship offer. When you do receive the offer, be very calm and think it through and talk it over with your parents or anyone else you trust. If you have questions or you don't understand the language of the offer, get help from the NCAA or other governing body.

It is very important that you understand the offer. The time to scrutinize the offer is before you sign it. Make sure the offer contains everything you were told you would be receiving.

Then, when you are satisfied that this is the program for you, sign the letter of intent, celebrate, and get ready to compete in college athletics.

THINGS YOU CAN DO

The more information recruiters and coaches can learn about you as an athlete, as a person, and as a student the more comfortable they will feel with their decision to offer you a scholarship. Chapter 7 will give you detailed information on what to include with your introductory letter, resume, and video.

1). Enlist the help of your high school coach or club coach. Many of these coaches played college sports and probably still have college contacts.

Telling them of your desire to play college sports might encourage them to mention you as a potential college athlete when scouts ask about talented high school athletes.

Some of these coaches will even call college coaches for you.

2). Phone the recruiting coach. Usually a college coach will remember and keep in mind a prospect that makes that first initial contact.

They are looking for student-athletes who want to be enrolled at their school and they are interested in talking to these prospects. Don't be shy, pick up the phone, and tell the coach that you are interested in finding out about athletic scholarship opportunities. Most likely your call will be appreciated.

3). Use the Internet. E-mail is an inexpensive yet effective way to let college coaches know of your interest in their programs.

In fact, some people have run their whole recruiting program by e-mail. Be sure to get the right coach and correct e-mail address. Log-on to the university's website, look for the athletic department and search for the sport and coach you want.

Be persistent, email the coach weekly. Let him know regularly of your continuing interest and of any new accomplishments, awards, etc.

4). Contract with a recruiting service. For one reason or another you may choose to utilize the services of one of these companies.

They offer a variety of specialties and marketing methods and usually charge a fee. Their job is to contact college coaches for you and lead you and your parents through the recruiting process. They can certainly save a lot of time and energy, but keep in mind you can do everything they can do. If you do decide to hire a recruiting service, make sure that you understand what it will provide. Ask questions about the service before you sign-up.

Some sample questions are: How successful percentage wise is your marketing service? Can you provide me with some references? Will I get an unbiased evaluation of my talent and skills? Does your service accept anybody or do you only accept players with the ability to play at the collegiate level?

If you decide to use one of these services, do your homework. How many student athletes have received scholarships using their programs?

You want to find out if they can deliver before you put down your money. Again, no one can guarantee that you will be offered an athletic scholarship. While you might choose to hire one of these companies, it is not necessary since this guide teaches you how to plan and execute your winning recruiting plan yourself.

If you do hire a recruiting service to help you develop and execute a marketing plan, maintain control yourself. Keep yourself informed of all efforts on your behalf.

FAQ

Should I wait for coaches to contact me? Many times good players sit and wait for the phone to ring. Some high school athletes feel that they would appear desperate and unwanted by other programs if they contacted a coach.
You could not be further from the truth. Coaches are extremely busy and actually are impressed by athletes who have the desire and guts to make the first move. Now this doesn't mean you are to pester the coaches out of their minds.

Can I have an agent? No, not while in high school or college.

Can I try out for a college team? Certain divisions have certain rules. Make sure you know the rules for the school that you are interested in.

What if I am contacted by a scouting service? NCAA rules prohibit scouting services from receiving payment based on the amount of your college scholarship. Be careful to make sure the scouting service meets the NCAA requirements.

When is it appropriate to ask a coach about an athletic scholarship? If you absolutely cannot attend college unless you have financial support, then explain this to interested coaches and find out if they are interested in you.

Where do college coaches recruit athletes? Coaches recruit from national, regional, and state level competitions, summer camps, athletes who have expressed an interest in their program, and recommendations received from alumni, and high school coaches. Will participating in multiple sports help me or hurt my scholarship opportunities? Many experts say, athletes are encouraged to work daily on the skills required for mastery in their chosen sport. Nevertheless, you can improve on some skills by participating in multiple sports.

If I am offered a scholarship during the early signing period, should I accept? If it is a school that you want to attend then go ahead and sign, because it will reduce the stress of recruiting on you and your family.
But remember to make sure this is the program and school for you. Once you sign the NLI there will be serious consequences if you change your mind.

What happens if I sign with a school and the head coach leaves the school? Since you signed with the school, you are bound to the school not to the coach.
Therefore, if the coach leaves after you have signed, you cannot go somewhere else without some kind of penalty.

What if a school I have never heard of shows interest in me? By all means, respond immediately. Check the school out, just because you haven't heard of it doesn't mean it isn't the perfect school for you.

Chapter 4
If You Want To Play Sports in College - Recruit The Coach!

Image Credit Photoxpress

Don't Wait To Be Contacted

Start checking out colleges and universities early. You need to be sure you are searching for the right school for you, not your parents, not your high school coach, your friends, etc.

You will be the one getting up, going to class, and going to practice. So, remember to choose a school because it is the school YOU want.

Via the Internet, some prospective colleges and universities offer virtual tours that give all kinds of information about the school and campus life.

Keep in mind that these virtual tours are created specifically as a marketing tool and will always promote only the positives. The first and most important thing you should be investigating at any prospective school is the academic program. Why, because, overwhelmingly, statistics indicate that most college athletes do not become professional athletes. Therefore, you will more than likely be depending on your college education to help you provide a good life for you and your family. Even if you are one of the rare "blue chip" players, you must still carefully consider the academic program.

When you are participating at the college level, there is a real possibility that you could receive a career ending injury. If you were attending the school only for the athletic program, would you be miserable if you could no longer play? Force yourself to think about the answers to these questions, and honestly consider which school will provide you with the best education. After you are comfortable with the academic program, then look into the athletic programs.

When you are satisfied with the academic and athletic programs, then research any other pertinent information concerning the school that might be of importance to you when it does come time to make your final decision. You might be interested in the location of the school, or the size of the school, or the size of the city the school is located, etc.

How would you feel if the coach who recruited you left the program while you were still playing?

There will be advantages and disadvantages to each bit of information concerning the school. Your senior year of high school will quite naturally be exciting. Not only will you be taking finals and thinking about graduation, but you will also probably still be playing on your varsity team, going to parties, proms, and other school events.

Set aside time during this hectic last year of high school to carefully evaluate and choose a college or university. Do your homework on each prospective school so you can make the very best decision for you. Crucial to receiving a scholarship at your school of choice is that your athletic and academic skills fit the school.

Look at the following guidelines for the different divisions. The more criteria that you meet in a particular division, the more likely you are to be qualified to compete successfully in that division.

To Compete at the NCAA Division I Level:
**Been actively recruited
**Been All-State, All Conference, or All-League Champion
**Qualified to compete at a junior or senior national meet
**Train, cross-train, or compete year round including weight/fitness training as part of your season and off-season program
**Participate in summer camps and tournaments that are known to have recruiters present.

To Compete at the NCAA Division II Level:
**Been a participant with a successful team program
**Competed at the regional level
**Trained in your sport seasonally, but have never gone beyond state competition

To Compete in NAIA:
**Been a participant with a successful team program
**Competed at the regional level
**Trained in your sport seasonally, but have never gone beyond state competition
**Usually looking for a smaller college or university with more emphasis on academics

To Compete at the NCAA Division III Level:
**Compete only during season at your high school
**Never qualified for state competition

To Compete at the NJCAA Level:
**Need more time to mature to the NCAA levels athletically?
**Need more time to improve academically
**Need more time to improve SAT & ACT scores
**Need more time to increase size, weight, height, etc...

If you are still not sure what division you should compete in, then you should check out schools from the different divisions.
You will get some feedback from the coaches that will help you to know where you fit athletically. If no coaches from Division I schools respond, then you will know that you are probably not a good athletic match for that division.

So, be sure to recruit different divisions since it will not only give you more opportunities, but it will also give you something to fall back on in case you don't get at scholarship at one of the Division I schools.

FAQ

What if I didn't play a particular sport in high school, but I want to play that sport at the college level? Check to see if the coaching staff will allow you to tryout to see if your level of ability is comparable to the existing athletes. Some schools will offer open tryouts to those students wanting to walk-on.

Questions Concerning the Academic Program
*What are the requirements for admission?
*Is there on campus housing?
*Is the major you are interested in offered?
*Is there a tutoring program?
*Is the school known more for its athletic or its academic programs?
*What size are the classes?
*What is the population of the city where the school is located?
*What is the cost of the school without a scholarship?
*How good is the department in your major?
*Are there career opportunities with this major/school?
*Is the school known as a party school?
*What percentage of players on scholarship graduate in four years?
*What type of academic support is offered through the institution?
*What is the average GPA of the teams?

Questions Concerning College Life and Location
*Is it close to home or far away?
*Would making visits home be a problem?
*Is the school in a nice area or is it in a high crime area?
*Do you like schools with a lot of tradition, or would you prefer one where you were able to be one of the people starting a new tradition?
*What is the weather like?
*What additional activities are available on and off campus?
*What kinds of employment opportunities are available?
*What condition and style are the residence halls? Coed dorms, suites or standard?
*Am I required to live on campus?

Questions Concerning the Athletic Program
*Do you like the coach? He/She will be a big part of your life

*Do you like the facilities where the team practices and plays? Are they new and impressive or do they look like something from a nightmare?

*Do you know any of the players on the team or know anything about them?

*Does the program have a scholarship available for your position?

*Does this school have an opening for your position? Are they looking for someone with your specific talents?

*Are you the approximate size, weight, strength and speed as other athletes that play your sport/position at that school?

*What would my physical requirements be? Gain weight, lose weight, etc.

*Are you a standout on your local team, conference, state or region?

*What is your level of skill versus the other players on the team?

*Does this program play the division level you should be in?

*What is the competition for your position like?

*Are any freshman, sophomore, junior or seniors already in line for the position you want?

*What does your future look like on the team?

*Are you competing with an All-American for playing time?

*How much playing time do you want?

*Would you rather play for a larger school and perhaps not have the opportunity to play often or play more frequently for a smaller school?

*Would you start immediately or be red-shirted?

*At your very best, would you be more of a support player than a star?

*Would you rather be a small fish in a big pond or a big fish in a small pond?

*When does the coach's contract end?

*Have the coach describe a typical day for a student-athlete.

*What are my opportunities for employment while I'm a student-athlete?

*Is financial aid available for summer school?

Chapter 5
What does a Full Ride College Athletic Scholarship Mean?

How Can an Academic Scholarship Help Me Get an Athletic Scholarship?
While there are several steps to obtaining an athletic scholarship, the actual process though often misunderstood is not as difficult as you may think.

If you have half way decent grades and you're an above average athlete you have an excellent chance of winning an athletic scholarship. Complete the steps as outlined in this guide and utilize the various links to organizations and other resources, as you need them.

Scholarships are forms of financial aid. They may be either athletic or academic, and either partial or full scholarships. Some, called "full-ride", provide for all expenses including tuition, books, board, room, equipment, uniforms, etc. Others provide for only one or two of your college expenses. Many provide for tuition only.

Scholarships are provided by a vast array of organizations, groups, schools, foundations, and individuals. This type of financial aid does not require repayment. A college education is usually the gateway to a successful future, but for most American families, it is also the largest single per child expense they will ever consider.

If you know that it will be a struggle for your family to provide for your college education, begin to search early in your junior year for the various types of financial aid that might be available to you. Also, you might qualify for one of the many scholarships that are awarded on merit or other certain criteria.

For Example, Wal-Mart provides a number of scholarships for children of Wal-Mart employees. If your GPA is high enough, it is very likely that you can qualify for some type of academic scholarship.

Seek the advice of your guidance counselor, but also check with some of your teachers, church and community leaders, your parents' employers, and the library.

Sometimes, guidance counselors though well intentioned, are not knowledgeable on all the scholarships available. Very often, due to the large number of students they are assigned, they just don't have the time to do an in-depth search for each student.

There are literally thousands of different types of scholarships requiring a variety of qualifications. Don't be discouraged if you don't immediately meet the qualifications for one. Just keep applying!

Many scholarships fail to be awarded simply because prospective students fail to apply. The main point to remember is that there is a lot of financial aid out there. Again, it is up to you to find it and apply for it. You should take charge of searching for and applying for these scholarships.

Please, for you own good, do not leave this very important matter in the hands of anyone else.

DO NOT WAIT UNTIL YOUR SENIOR YEAR TO START YOUR SCHOLARSHIP SEARCH!

Many of these scholarships are awarded early. If you do get an academic scholarship, you will increase your chances of receiving an athletic scholarship. While it is illegal for NCAA coaches to call you or to return phone calls from you until July 1 of your senior year, you can call and contact them as many times as you like. Use this rule to your advantage by contacting the coaches in your junior year. This is an opportunity for you to be pro-active in your recruiting game plan.

All NCAA Division I member schools offer athletic scholarships based on one-year awards that can be renewed on an annual basis up to five years and within a six-year period of time.

Renewal is not guaranteed and may be dependent upon meeting academic and athletic minimum requirements. The different types of

scholarships and the terminology used when talking about them
follow:

Full Athletic Scholarship or sometimes called a "Full Ride": This
type of scholarship covers all college expenses including books,
tuition, and room and board (means and a dorm room). There are not
many of these "full ride" scholarships available to incoming first
year students.

Academic Scholarships can cover everything including tuition,
books, and room, and board; or, it could provide for only a portion of
these expenses.

In some states, if you score high enough on the ACT or SAT you
may be eligible for a tuition scholarship paid for by the state. As we
said before, there are literally thousands of different types of
academic scholarships.

Get all of your scholarship research completed during your junior
year so that you can be ready to apply at the beginning of your senior
year. Develop a tracking sheet for when to apply for these
scholarships. They will all have different deadlines. Avoid missing
one by staying organized.

>>>Coaches will always try to stretch scholarship money as far as
possible. For example, let's say that you have maintained a good
high school GPA and have also scored well on the SAT or ACT; in
fact, you have scored well enough to qualify for an academic
scholarship that will cover your tuition.

There are other athletes who have applied for the same athletic
scholarship who do not have the high scores and GPA that you do.
Knowing this, the coach has just narrowed his decision, and if all
other things are equal, you will be awarded a partial athletic
scholarship, which will pay all your expenses except your tuition.
Your academic scholarship combined with your partial athletic
scholarship will essentially act as a "full ride" scholarship. Together
they will provide for all your college expenses.>>> This situation is
a no-brainer; the coach will choose you hands down, because he
doesn't have to spend as much of his budget in order to sign you.
This is just one of many examples of why academics are so
important.

Partial scholarships cover only a part of college expenses. Tuition may be covered, but not books, room but not board.

Athletic scholarships monies are usually limited; therefore, the coach divides the funds he has available. As in the example above, the idea is to use the athletic scholarship budget in a way that will get the most and best talent for the available money.

If you do receive a partial scholarship, you might need to consider and try securing other forms of financial aid.

In order to receive other forms of financial aid, you must complete a financial form known as the FAFSA (Free Application for Student Aid).

If you need financial aid, apply early. There are many, many academic grants, scholarships, and loans that go unclaimed each and every year. Click Financial Tips for more info.

Depending on certain coaches, budgets, and school policy some sports do not typically give incoming freshmen athletic scholarships.

Walk-On is a student/athlete who does not receive athletic aid. Walk-on opportunities are available at every level of play for every sport at every school.

There are preferred, invited, and uninvited walk-on situations. Walk-ons are treated differently from school to school. The best thing to do in this situation is ask the coach at the specific school you are attending and find out their policy regarding walk-ons.

A walk-on must successfully prove that he or she can perform at a level that will increase the success of the program. The walk-on is typically a person who has the ability and also the sincere desire to play collegiate sports, however, he lacks the required skill level.

Another example of a walk-on is an athlete that signed with another university and did not fulfill his or her obligation to that school; therefore the student-athlete would be ineligible to receive financial aid from any other school for a stipulated amount of time.

Many coaches actively recruit walk-ons to supplement their roster. A walk-on receives the same beneficial treatment that the scholarship athletes do including preferential registration status, class scheduling, and housing.

If you do walk-on, the potential is usually there to obtain financial aid after your freshman year providing you can prove to the coach that you are as good if not better than the scholarship players.

In-State vs. Out-of-State Tuition

Whether you are an in state or an out-of-state student-athlete makes a big difference in the cost of education. The state supported schools typically offer lower tuition cost to student-athletes who are residents of the state where the school is located.

Out-of-state tuition is often significantly more expensive than in-state tuition; and, of course it is more expensive to recruit an out-of-state athlete due to traveling cost, phone cost, etc.

So, if a coach has a limited budget and most of them do, he or she can get more bang for the buck by recruiting in-state student-athletes.

Remember, though, that some programs don't have the financial resources to bring in athletes from out of state no matter how much they might want to get them to campus.

If you are interested in attending and playing for one of these schools, you will have to make it your business to travel to the school at your expense.

FAQ:

Can an academic scholarship help me get an Athletic Scholarship? Yes

What is Title IX? Basically, Title IX is the federal law that was passed and implemented to guarantee women the same financial and other benefits granted to men in college athletics.

Does Title IX take away from male athletes? No, however, most men's athletic departments would argue that point. College football is excluded from Title IX, but all other college athletic programs are supposed to be treated equally.

If I am attending a university on an academic scholarship, how do I go about trying to join the team? Make an appointment with the coach and inform him/her of your desire to compete for the university.

After my first year of collegiate play, will my athletic scholarship automatically be renewed? Scholarships are one-year contracts. However, coaches don't recruit athletes to keep them for only one year.

They have recruited you because they need your talent for their program. Your contract will most likely be renewed from year to year unless you don't measure up to what the coach thought you would. If you keep your nose clean, keep your GPA acceptable, and play to your potential you should be fine.

Chapter 6
Your Game Plan to Play College Sports

Since you now know what your strengths and weaknesses are better than anyone, your mission is to MAXIMIZE YOUR STRENGTHS and minimize or eliminate your weaknesses.

Stay energized and focused each step of the way. Candidly evaluate your progress and be organized in your pursuit. Develop a "never give up" and "never give in attitude".

Accomplish your game plan with intensity of purpose and stick with it until you have the scholarship in hand. Constantly look for ways to improve athletically and academically so that you can give the recruiters and coaches every reason to choose you. Generally, college coaches start looking at recruits somewhere between the spring of the junior year and the summer before their senior year of high school.

Academically Refer to Chapter 9 to make sure you are taking the required courses for the division you want to participate in.

As Soon As Possible: With your future in mind, consistently work to keep your grades up. Develop good, daily study habits that will serve you well on into college. Also, make and accomplish on a regular basis new and bigger athletic goals. Consciously strive to improve in both areas. Plan and follow a schedule, which provides time for family life, social activities, academics and athletics. It will be crucial that you learn to balance these areas of your life before you arrive at college.

Many, many college freshmen flunk out in the first year because they have not learned how to balance their daily activities. Be willing to discipline yourself socially. Decisions that you make even at this point can affect your chance for a scholarship. Remember, if it comes down to you and someone else with the same athletic talent, the scholarship will go to the one with better academics and better attitude. You may ask why do coaches care about my GPA? In your mind, you may be thinking that my GPA, no matter what it is, won't affect my contribution to the team. You couldn't be more wrong.

Your high school GPA is an important indicator coaches use to determine your possible success in college, your maturity level, and your degree of self-discipline.

If you were failing high school, why would a coach believe you could succeed in college? Additionally, once you receive a scholarship you will have to maintain your GPA in college to maintain your eligibility.

Academically - Sophomore

Spring - Set your goals as to what you expect of yourself as well as what is expected of you to be eligible. Talk to your academic counselor at school and inform him or her of your goals.

Very often a counselor can offer suggestions and tips to help insure your success. Visit the career center and start researching colleges you want to attend and check out their admission requirements.

Focus on what you will need to do to accomplish these goals. Pay attention to your studies, keep your grades up and make sure you are on track to meet all eligibility requirements.

Plan out your schedule for your junior year and try to balance your time. Schedule time for academics, athletics, family and extracurricular activities.

In order to improve in all areas of academics, you will need to plan to study for every test. Then the actual test will be the easy part. Remember the one test you don't study for could make the difference in where or if you go to college on scholarship.

Athletically - Sophomore

Summer - Set goals as to what you want to accomplish this year as well as your junior and senior season. Then make a list of what you will need to do to accomplish these goals.

One exercise that is very beneficial is to write out an athletic resume. Make this resume cover a list of all that you have thus far accomplished athletically.

Next, write a resume covering all you want to accomplish by next year at this time. Then, list the things that you will need to do to accomplish these goals. Begin researching what schools you would like to play for. Try to go to some of their games, or watch them on television, watch ESPN, read about them in the newspaper.

Academically - Junior Year
Fall - This year is key to building your recruiting foundation. There are approximately 1975 colleges and universities in this country with athletic programs.

Request some general information from the office of admissions at the schools you are interested in throughout the United States to get a complete listing of possible schools.

Get an ACT/SAT study guide and start studying for these important exams. ACT/SAT preparation help is abundant and is quickly available on the Internet.

Also, you might talk to other students who have taken the test before you.
Remember, based on your ACT/SAT scores you could qualify for some form of academic scholarship that would make you even more attractive to college coaches.

Winter - Stay on course, keep up and study for all tests.

Spring - Register, prepare and take your ACT/SAT tests. You can't participate in college athletics if you don't take the exam, or if you take the exam and don't score high enough.
In fact, if you don't take this exam and score high enough, not only will you not get to participate in college sports, you won't even get into college. Taking and passing the test is your responsibility - step up and do it. You might ask why you need to take the ACT/SAT now?

College coaches want to make sure you make an acceptable score before they will consider making a scholarship offer to you. Help them keep you in mind by staying eligible? Also, you need to leave yourself time to retake the test in case you have a bad test day for one reason or another. For example, girlfriend/boyfriend troubles keep you from concentrating and giving the test your best shot. You would be wise to take the ACT/SAT two or three times since your scores can improve 10% - 40% just by retaking the test. Don't wait until spring of your senior year to take the ACT/SAT-it is an unnecessary pressure and could very possibly cost you a scholarship.

Summer - Plan out your senior schedule and make sure you are doing all the things necessary to be eligible for college. Fill out all academic and financial types of scholarship forms you can get your hands on.
Learn what types of scholarships other than athletic are available. Apply, apply, and apply! In many cases based on financial need, the first ones that apply receive the financial scholarship. Your academic counselor can assist you with this.

Athletically - Junior
Fall - Start contacting coaches from the various schools that you are interested in. Send the coaches a basic letter expressing your interest in their programs and also include your game schedule.
This is the best way to get noticed, as well as to find out what it will take to be a part of his or her program. Put the finishing touches on your resume, video and other materials that you will be sending to coaches when they express interest.

DURING SEASON: Think and play your sport like never before, you will need to focus on being the best student of the game, the best athlete in the game and the athlete who plays with impeccable sportsmanship. In general, during this season of play, be the best that you can be. Keep articles out of newspapers and keep track of any honors you receive. Accumulate any pertinent information that separates you from the crowd.

OFF-SEASON: Reevaluate your goals for your senior season. Look at what you had hoped to accomplish and what you actually did accomplish. Rewrite your goals for this season. Continue following and researching the teams that you are interested in.

Academically – Senior

Fall - Register and be certified by the NCAA Initial-Eligibility Clearinghouse, your counselors can obtain registration materials, at no cost by calling the clearinghouse at 319-337-1492 or you can register on line at http://www.ncaaclearinghouse.net/.

At this time, a transcript, which includes six semesters of grades, should be sent to the clearinghouse from the high school. You must fill out the NCAA Initial Eligibility form to be eligible to compete in college athletics; the fee is $30.00.

Make sure that you're meeting all deadlines for any scholarship and grant applications. Keep checking to see if there are any other scholarships you qualify for. It's important to make sure that you have the applications to each school you're interested in.

Start filling out the applications as soon as possible. Schedule enough time to work on the applications; it will be time consuming. Begin to think about what you'll write your essays about.

Stay in contact with your college guidance counselors. They can help you honestly evaluate your chances of being admitted to each school on your list.

Take at least three SAT II's. Many colleges have SAT II requirements. If you're not happy with your junior year scores, keep taking the test until your scores are acceptable.

Remember, colleges look very closely at first semester grades from this year. Avoid any senior year slump.

Winter- Stay on task with your studies. This is crucial. Study and prepare, remember one test can make the difference. There will be many extra activities this year. To do well, you'll have to maintain a balanced yet challenging schedule. Follow-up on your applications and make sure nothing else needs to be done to be eligible for any scholarship. It is your responsibility to stay informed and organized during this process. Use a tracking sheet for the applications.

Athletically - Senior

DURING SEASON: This is when the cream rises to the top and this is when all your hard work starts to become apparent. Continue your pattern of excellence. If you have done all that you should have, this year should be one of the most exciting years of your life.

This doesn't necessarily mean that you will be the next superstar at the top school in the country, but it does mean that you'll have an excellent shot at getting an athletic scholarship.

OFF-SEASON: Follow-up with all coaches and make sure they have everything they need. Make sure the coaches know you are interested; however don't make a pest out of yourself.

WAYS TO IMPROVE Academically

If you are struggling in any class, get a tutor. Your academic counselor can refer you to someone. Not only is your grade in that particular class important as far as your GPA is concerned, but that class is very likely a building block for the more advanced required college course.

For example, it you are having difficulty with high school math, now is the time to establish your math foundation, do not wait until you get to college. If a tutor is not
practical, then joining study groups with other students can be very helpful.

If you are in the habit of studying only the night before a test, determine to change to the much more productive schedule of studying on a daily basis. You will perform better, learn more and actually spend less time overall in studying. Don't skip school or be excessively tardy since these behaviors are indicators of your ability to take responsibility and your level of maturity.

While the coach's job is to recruit the best athletic talent, they must also make every effort to make sure that every recruit can perform academically. If you can't maintain the required GPA, you won't be allowed to play.

WAYS TO IMPROVE - Athletically

**Attention baseball, soccer, softball, swimming, and track participants. If you are interested in getting an athletic scholarship, it is probably more important for you to play club sports if you are interested in playing at the Division I or Division II schools. Coaches in these sports recruit heavily from the clubs.

CAMPS: Coaches spend summers coaching at camps and interacting with athletes for the purpose of recruiting. Most coaches run camps on their own campuses and if they're not running one, you can bet they are working some other coach's camp.

Participating in camps is highly recommended and is a great way to compete against different athletes, learn new skills, improve skills and get exposure. There are a variety of summer camps offered. Attend as many as possible. If the financing for the camp will be a hardship, contact the coach in charge and ask if there is anything you can do to get a scholarship for the camp or work at the camp in some capacity.

AAU: Amateur Athletic Union charters teams from coast to coast in thirty-two sports and in a number of age groups. AAU competitions allow athletes to compete with other similarly talented athletes throughout the country and it is one very effective way to get that all-important coach exposure. Multiple coaches can see an athlete during one of these AAU competitions. Shoe and gear companies such as Nike, Adidas and Reebok spend millions of dollars on these AAU competitions. They provide sponsorships to high school teams, AAU teams and college teams. The sponsorship can include free shoes, camps, clothing and gear. It is perfectly legal for athletes to be steered toward colleges that AAU coaches suggest however there is an ethical controversy concerning the influence AAU coaches and shoe companies have on athletes. The NCAA is currently discussing reducing the number of days that athletes can be recruited in the summer because of alleged recruiting improprieties. Click www.ncaa.org for the latest NCAA ruling.

CLUB SPORTS: There are only a few sports that offer year-round club teams: volleyball, softball, swimming, soccer and baseball, to name a few. Club sports are for the most part expensive, but if you have the opportunity to participate with a club team, it is highly recommended. Many college coaches, especially women's and men's soccer coaches, rely heavily upon scouting club teams to fill their rosters.

College coaches believe that club players are more dedicated and talented since they play year round and are constantly involved with their sport.

Therefore, if it is possible for you to participate in club sports, you will be constantly improving your game and at the same time be increasing your chance of getting noticed.

COORDINATION: The way you move, balance, change of direction, and how smoothly or fluidly you perform your physical skills is called coordination. Coordination is very important to any athlete, without it, you can forget it. With excellent coordination you can become an outstanding athlete. Coordination is a gift from God, however you can improve your coordination by participating in as many athletic movements as you can. Coordination can be improved beginning in childhood and continuing through high school. Each sport, no matter how different, can teach your body how to fine-tune your coordination.

STRENGTH: Today more than ever, strength is an advantage in most if not all sports. Strength is a great asset but it is not measured the way most people think. Recruiters and coaches don't focus on how much weight you can lift. They want to see how you use your strength on the field or court. Do you appear to be physically stronger than your opponents or are you pushed around? Are you easily knocked off balance? What your strength looks like on the court, in the water or on the field is what is important.

CONDITIONING AND STAMINA: There is not much worse than being tired and having to do something. So how do you prevent this? Easy, get in shape and stay in shape. Being in good condition is essential to your success.

There are numerous reasons why being in shape is advantageous.
1) You are less likely to be injured.
2) You'll be able to play your very best at all times.
3) It's possible that a scout or recruiter could be watching or videotaping you.
4) Being in tip-top condition shows that you are a disciplined athlete who is willing to do what it takes to be the very best.

If you get tired because you aren't in good condition, think about the message you're probably sending to the scouts and recruiters. Among other things, you're telling them that you are not quite as fast or don't jump quite as high or swim quite as strong as someone they might be interested in.

They are interested in the bottom line only. If someone lacks the dedication and discipline to get in and stay in shape, chances are that he or she won't work very hard at anything else. Bottom line--GET IN SHAPE AND STAY THAT WAY IF YOU WANT AN ATHLETIC SCHOLARSHIP!!

In summary, participate in camps as often as possible. Compete with many different athletes, don't just round up the people who you know you can beat.
The better your competition, the more you will improve. Make it a point to play at higher and higher levels. As an example, if you're on a women's basketball team, use a good men's team as a practice squad.

Become a student of the game, watch and learn from athletes who are better than you and practice what they do. Constantly work on skills and drills to improve your strength, coordination, and conditioning.

WAYS TO IMPROVE Personally Always be polite and courteous to all coaches (high school and college), officials, and counselors. These people can make you or break you in the years to come.

Why is this so? Very often, a coach will narrow his decision for a particular scholarship down to three people. If their athletic skills are approximately equal, then character attributes will be of prime consideration. When you're actually being seriously considered for an athletic scholarship, college coaches and recruiters will be talking to your high school counselors, coaches, teammates, teachers and anyone else who they feel will help give them an accurate picture of your overall character and accomplishments.

Again, treat all of these people with respect and do your best in your interactions with them; give them every reason to speak well of you. Be aware that coaches move around a lot. Just because a coach is employed at a school you're not interested in this year, does not mean that he or she won't relocate to the school of your choice next year.

Don't rule out anyone anywhere; keep your options open, that way you will have more and better opportunities. As we stated earlier, if it comes down to a decision between two athletes who are of equal athletic ability, the scholarship will go to the one who has performed better academically and who has a better attitude. Stay out of trouble and avoid drugs. Think of the people you admire and the qualities you admire about them. Then try to emulate those qualities. Stay positive and don't tear other athletes down in an effort to make yourself look better. The lists below contain some popular character traits and other qualities that coaches look for when making decisions concerning scholarships.

Do you possess these personal characteristics? If you are an above average athlete and possess most of these characteristics, you will have an excellent chance to succeed in college athletics.

Take the time right now to measure how you rate relative to each of these personal traits.
*Drive
*Aggressiveness
*Determination
*Conscientiousness
*Self-motivated
*Trust
*Leadership
*Respectful
*Disciplined
*Emotional Control
*Hard-working
*Team Oriented
*Competitiveness
*Mental Toughness

*Outgoing
*Committed to excellence
*Positive attitude
*Responsibility
*Coachability

FAQ

Do I need to register with the NCAA-Clearinghouse if I have been home-schooled? If you have been home schooled during all of grades nine through twelve, you do not have to register with the clearinghouse. Your certification status will be determined through an initial-eligibility waiver.

If you attended a " traditional" school for some portion of grades nine through twelve, you are required to register with the NCAA Clearinghouse.
Will the NCAA Clearinghouse provide the eligibility information to the colleges that are recruiting me? No, You will have to request the NCAA Clearinghouse to send the information to the specific colleges you want to receive the information.

Chapter 7
Phone Calls, Letters and Emails

Before you are able to sell yourself to others you must be able to sell you to you! Does that make sense? Keeping this idea in mind and before you go any further, list five qualities that set you apart from your competition.

Examples might be: leadership abilities, fundamental soundness, strength, size, quickness, speed, high GPA, coachability, desire, heart, work ethic, and commitment to winning. This is the time to reach down to your gut level and list your strengths honestly.

This is not the time to become over confident and say that you have an eight-foot vertical jump or anything else that is not true. Any untruth will certainly come back to haunt you.

Include only those accomplishments and attributes that can be backed up by documentation or third party reference.

Part of your promotional campaign should include recommendations from your high school coach, personal coach, or club coach. And, hopefully their assessment of your abilities will back up the profile you've already sent to the college coach.

If one of your high school coaches is inclined to assist you in the recruiting process, you're in luck and it can be a terrific advantage to you.

Some are willing, even anxious to help while others are not. Some have been college athletes themselves and know what to do to help and will also feel more comfortable in this roll. If you are fortunate enough to have one of these coaches, be respectful of their time.

They will very often make phone calls, write letters of recommendation, and even accompany you on college visits. He or she can be of tremendous help to you; however, remember they don't get paid to secure your athletic scholarship and you should continue doing everything you can to nail it down yourself.

Many other high school coaches are at the opposite end of the continuum and do very little to assist student-athletes. They won't make phone calls, write recommendations or make contacts for you.

If you have one of these coaches, while it does make your job a little more difficult, don't be discouraged, it's just another hurdle to jump, and you can still succeed without these people.

Look around for other people who would be willing to help like: a club coach, personal coach, or perhaps even a high school administrator who used to be a coach. As an aside, there are a few self-serving high school coaches that are hoping to promote themselves along with their star athletes.

These coaches might encourage an athlete to choose a program that is more beneficial to the coach than it is to the athlete. These coaches are hoping to move up to the world of college athletics along with their outstanding athletes.
After playing for such a coach, I am sure that you will readily recognize what his or her ultimate motives are. Just think for yourself. What program is best suited to you? Select that program. This chapter will show you how to develop the various components of your recruiting campaign. It will also teach you how to use each component and how to use them together as a marketing package.

These tools can all be used effectively to gain exposure to college coaches. Since you've done the preliminary self-evaluation, you know that you have the physical, mental, and academic skills to play at the college level.

Now all you need to do is get yourself discovered. You'll want to manage your campaign skillfully, remain vigilant, and constantly monitor your progress. The tracking sheet is a necessary tool to keep you organized and on schedule.

TRACKING SHEET
Make a tracking sheet similar to the one below to keep track of all contacts and materials sent to college recruiters and coaches.

Begin the sheet with your very first contact and note all follow-up materials and contacts. Make a folder for each school you're recruiting. Get yourself a big calendar with room on each day to write what needs to be done on that day. Use this or any other method to keep your recruiting campaign organized. You will be following up with some of these coaches every couple of weeks. Every time you follow-up, have some reason to be making the follow-up contact.

For example, you're playing in an upcoming tournament, received an award, forwarding a game schedule. It can be anything, just have some reason to call or write.

CONTACT/MATERIALS TRACKING SHEET
School Coach Phone # Sent/Called Notes Make a list of fifty - sixty schools you where you would be interested in playing and attending. Include on the list schools from different NCAA Divisions, NAIA as well as NJCAA. Also include on the list a couple schools where you are pretty sure you can get in.

It is vital that you recruit schools from the different divisions right up until you sign on the dotted line. Why? You want to keep all your options open and anything can happen.
For example: several top name schools are recruiting you early in the season and then you blow out a knee. The big schools will reconsider their offers on this news and you'll be glad that you have other options to fall back on.

You want to compete at the highest level you can, but you also want to secure an athletic scholarship. If you know you're not Division I material, don't waste your time or the coach's time.

Recruiting a wide range of schools will give you the best chance to succeed in your pursuit. Inform yourself about each school, do your homework on both its athletic program and its academic program.

Compiling this list will take a little time, however, the Internet will make the research easier and much less time consuming.Academics should be your primary consideration. While there are 360 thousand

NCAA athletes, only 150 go on to play professional football and only 50 go on to play professional basketball each year.

These figures are staggering and should give you a reality check. The vast majority of college athletes do not go on to play professional sports. Your first goal should be to prepare yourself for life, so there's no point of including a school on your list that doesn't offer the major you're seeking.

Imagine playing your sport at that school. If you can see yourself as an athlete at the school, imagine that you unfortunately received a career ending injury, would you still be happy at the school? From this list of schools, select from ten to twenty that will be your top choices. Initiate phone calls to recruiting coaches at these schools. You'll be sending introductory letters and profiles out to all the schools, but these school that are your top picks will have priority status and get extra attention.

PHONE CALLS

The phone call puts you in the system. A good phone call from you makes a big impression and it puts you squarely in the driver's seat of your recruiting process.

With these phone calls you become proactive in recruiting the coaches. College coaches know they can appear intimidating to student-athletes.

When you take the initiative to make that first phone call, you're demonstrating to them that you have drive and guts and that you're not afraid to go after what you want.

These are qualities they like to see in their athletes. So, suck it up and make those calls, you'll stand out from the crowd with this strategy. A phone call to a college coach from your high school coach or some other reputable person will also draw favorable attention.

Many college coaches lack the time, staff, and funding to recruit extensively.

They often settle into a routine of recruiting close to home and using a known network of high school coaches and other college coaches for new recruits.

For this reason, unless you are proactive in the game of recruiting, your talent may go undiscovered. Use the phone call to introduce yourself and to get yourself in the recruiting system.

Remember, while the ultimate goal to your recruiting program is to secure an athletic scholarship, you first must gain college coach exposure. Whether you make the phone calls or someone else makes them in your behalf, do not call a coach on game day. Go to the school's website, look for the game schedule, print it out, keep it in that school's folder.

The website will also be your source for the Athletic Department's phone number or maybe even the number for the coach you're trying to contact. When you make your first call, be courteous and to the point. Do not come across as arrogant or ignorant. A secretary who is paid to screen the coach's calls will probably answer your call. You will more than likely not get to talk to the coach on this first call, but you or whoever is calling on your behalf will be able to leave a message designed to pique his or her interest. For example, if it is a basketball program, you might say, I'm Lisa Brown and I play point guard for Little Rock Central. Our record this year was 22 and 2. I'm very impressed with your basketball program and would like to find out if my talents would fit your program needs at this time. Also ask if you can send your profile and or a video.

If someone else makes the call, he or she can "magnify your horn a little louder". They might say something like: "I've got a point guard who averages 24 pts. a game and I think she would be a perfect fit for your program. She is very impressed with your basketball program and would be interested in playing there." In either case, be sure to leave your contact information (name and phone number and best time to reach you). This last kind of message will find its way to the appropriate coach in short order. If you haven't heard back from the coach in two weeks, call back. They are all very busy and most of them are well intentioned.

They may have intended to call, lost your phone number or whatever. This second call from you may just motivate them to action.

Be persistent until you get to talk to the coach. Once you do establish phone contact with the coach, you can use the phone as one method to keep the coach updated on your interest and accomplishments.

If you are able to talk to the coach on this first call, be polite and to the point. Express an interest in playing for his or her program and ask about scholarship opportunities.

Be yourself, organized and prepared to answer the coach's questions. Your ACT/SAT scores will most certainly come up. The coach will be able to tell from this first phone call whether he wants more information from you.

If he/she is interested in learning more about you, he/she will send you a form letter, questionnaire, school catalog and possibly other materials. Comply promptly with all requests. If he/she is not interested in you, don't be discouraged or demoralized. His lack of interest may have nothing to do with you; he simply may not have a need for your talent at this time. Take this opportunity to ask the coach if he knows of a school that might be interested in you. This coach networks with other coaches and he might be able to refer you to the coach who can use your talent.

Remember this is a numbers game. Keep making the calls, the next one could be the perfect fit. Make a note to thank the coach for his time.

LETTERS TO COACHES These introductory letters are unsolicited letters used to get you into each school's recruiting system. You can't be offered a scholarship if you're not noticed to the point of getting in the system.

These letters are an important component of your recruiting campaign. Early in your junior year, send introductory letters to all the colleges and universities on your list even if you have already talked to the coach by phone.

The hard working secretaries and assistants will see that your letter accomplishes its purpose. Your letter will probably generate a form-letter response and a questionnaire. That's exactly what it is supposed to do, just get the ball rolling by gaining the initial recognition from the coach.

1) Make a list of fifty to sixty colleges and universities that you have selected to recruit.

2) Find out who the head coaches are and address letters to them with the correct spelling of their names and titles. Using their correct titles and spelling their names correctly is a mark of respect. Do your homework on each school and coach. Never just say, ""Dear Coach". Additionally, be sure to include the name of the college in the letter. Don't just write I am interested in your school. Express your interest in their program and school and also mention that you are interested in finding out about scholarship opportunities.

3). Be sure to include a schedule of your upcoming high school games or inform them that you will send one as soon as it becomes available. Also include any information about camps you will be attending or tournaments you will be playing in.

4). Include your academic assessment (academic transcript, ACT/SAT scores, GPA, class rank, special honors) and your athletic achievements and honors.
All of this information should be provided in terms that are easily identifiable by the coach (records held, championships won, tournaments participated in, and teams played for). You should also provide the name and current status of your high school coach.

5). This letter should be one page in length and is meant to be only an introduction, not a detailed summary of all your awards and abilities, however you should make every effort to make sure your letter stands out from the majority of letters received by the coach. Make your letter useful to the coach. First it should include your academic transcript and ACT or SAT scores. If your documentation shows that you meet the academic guidelines for his school, he will most likely make a mental note to keep tabs on you and watch your video when it arrives.

6). Thank the coach for taking the time to read your letter.
SAMPLE INTRODUCTORY LETTER May 5th, 2012
Mr. Jim Brown
Head Basketball Coach
Department of Athletics
University of North America
University Town, USA 54321
Dear Coach Brown,
My name is Fred Jones. I'm currently a junior at Little Rock Central High School in Little Rock, AR. The enclosed unofficial transcript shows my GPA to be 3.55 in my core classes. My SAT scores so far are a combined ll30. I plan to retake the test this year in an effort to improve my scores. I am a 6'2", 195 lb. Point guard, and will be a starter for the third year this season. I was All-State last year and also received my school's MVP award. My averages this past year was: 23 pts. 11 assists, 5 rebounds, and 5 steals. Last summer, I attended the basketball camp at the University of Memphis. My evaluation from that camp is enclosed. I' interested in attending another camp this next summer and would like to have more information about yours. You can contact my current high school coach, Mr. John Smith at 501-555-5555 concerning my athletic abilities and personal characteristics. I would like to receive any information about your program and scholarship opportunities. My contact information is as follows: 2222 S. Olive St., Little Rock, AR 77777. I can be reached at 901-555-0000 usually after 3:00 p.m.
Sincerely,
Scott Jones

This letter is very useful to the coach. After reading this letter, he will more than likely add you to his recruiting system. Why? You've provided him a copy of your transcript with your ACT/SAT scores on it.
If they are not included on the transcript, make a copy of them and enclose the copy with the letter. With your academic documentation in hand, he now mentally puts you down as a possible recruit.

Once you receive information back from the college coach, prepare a packet with the following information:
1. Athletic Profile with two pictures (one should be a full shot sport picture).
2. Athletic Accomplishments and Honors.
3. Current High School Game Schedule.
4. Personal Information including college aspirations.
5. Letters of recommendation from coaches.
6. Academic Profile.
7. Video (if requested).

RESUME
All of the above information numbers one through seven are components of your resume. Each topic one through seven can be a separate page.
You may not have enough data to fill up a page for each topic, in that case, condense what you have, but do include pertinent information from each item.

Be creative with the resume and make every effort to make it attractive, professional, and interesting. How the coach perceives you depends on how you well you put this package together.

The resume is critical to helping you stand apart and above the crowd. One of the key objectives of the resume is to make you look good.
This is a legitimate opportunity to do a little bragging, however, be honest with the coach and be able to back up anything you've stated.

If you are a swimmer or track athlete be sure to include best times in specific events. Football players include your time in the 40, and basketball players include your vertical jump.

1. Athletic Profile: Give more details about you and your sport. Position, height, weight, hand preference, age, birth date, running speed, batting average, average points scored, vertical jump, (your statistics in your sport), other sports played, GPA, SAT/ACT scores, class rank. Affix your picture to this page. You want to grab the coach's attention on this page.

2. Athletic Accomplishments and Honors: Include any records held and all honors received. Start with your freshman year and list through the present time all of your athletic awards (Special Awards, Tournament Awards, All-State, All-City, Captain, Scholar Athlete, etc.).

3. Current High School Game Schedule: If you don't have one yet, send it as soon as it becomes available. The coach will need as much time as possible to schedule a visit to one of your games.

4. Personal Information Including College Aspirations: The coach not only wants to know about your athletic background, but he or she also wants to know about you, the other person you are when you're not participating in sports. The recruiting coach will be checking with several other people as to your background and character.

Administrators, teachers, counselors, other coaches, ministers, other parents and anyone else who might be able to vouch for your character could be contacted. This investigation into your background is all a routine part of the recruiting process. The coach is just trying to make sure that you are a good risk and that you will have an excellent chance to succeed at the collegiate level. List your extracurricular accomplishments (Honor roll, club and student offices held, National Honor Roll, community service, church, etc.)

Your involvement in activities other than athletics demonstrates that you have learned how to balance your time. It shows that you are well rounded and that you are probably a good candidate to succeed at the college level. Include in this section a personal statement of your goals, dreams, and commitments.

5. Letters Of Recommendation From High School Coaches: College coaches use these letters as one method to verify the information you've provided on your profile. One or two will be enough.

Be sure to provide your high school coach, club coach, or whomever you've asked for a reference the correctly spelled name and complete address of the college coach he is writing to. The address should include the name, title, school, street address or P.O. Box number, City, State, and zip. The reference letter should include a brief history of his/her experience with you, his current position, an overview of your accomplishments (this should back up anything you've already said about yourself academically, athletically and personally), reasons why he/she is recommending that you be considered for the coach's college athletic program, and he/she should also be sure to include their phone number in case the coach has additional questions.

Over all, the tone of this letter should be complimentary to you and should vouch for you in every way. Some tips for securing great reference letters are:
* Make writing the letter easy to write. In addition to the correct spelling and so forth, include with your request some of the information you've provided on your profile such as your statistics and honors.
* Write a thank you note to the reference writer.
* Give ample time for the recommendation to be completed.
* Avoid asking anyone who will be unable to write a favorable letter.
* Ask for the letter when the writer is in a good frame of mind.
* Never have a family member write the letter unless he or she happens to be your high school coach.
* If you ask for a reference letter from your high school coach or club coach and you're turned down, just block it out and go on to someone else. Unfortunately, some people have the misguided idea that if you're good enough to play college sports, the college recruiting coaches will find you. This is simply not true. Don't make the mistake of trusting your dreams to this erroneous mentality. In fact, you will be helping the coaches and yourself by contacting them first.

6. Academic Profile Provide an academic transcript. Usually your ACT/SAT scores will be on the transcript, if not, make a copy and attach. Include your GPA, class rank (if available), and any special academic honors. This part of the resume is important to the coach.

If your academics are good and you're also a good athlete you've moved up a notch on his/her list of potential recruits.

7. Videos A video has many advantages. It doesn't lie and it actually shows the prospective coach what your skill level is. He or she has read your resume with all of its documentation, seen your pictures, and might possibly have already talked to your high school coach. The video is the most powerful and essential weapon in your recruiting arsenal as it gives the coach the opportunity to view your skill level in a game situation. It's the next best thing to seeing you play in person. The video cuts expenses for the coach since he doesn't have to travel to actually see you play. If you live and play a hundred miles up the road from the coach, travel expenses wont come into play that much, but if you live a across the country, they would certainly be a major consideration.

(Remember the easier you make it for a coach to see you the better). You don't necessarily have to have a professional video, however you do want the coach to be able to make out what is happening. So what should be in this all-important video?

1) The beginning of the tape should include a brief personal introduction that gives your height, weight, high school, GPA, ACT/SAT scores, position, home address and home phone number. Be very sincere and tell the coach that you are interested in participating in college athletics and are particularly interested in his or her program. Thank them for their time and tell them you look forward to hearing from them soon.

2) The next section should consist of 5-10 minutes of edited footage showing as many different aspects of your game as possible, try also to edit out as much non-action as possible.

3) This last section should consist of 10-15 minutes of unedited footage, which shows how you really match up against your competition. Choose video footage where you were great, good and fair. If you just choose footage where you are great, they may think you are trying to fool them.

OK--so what if you are not able to send this type of tape. Relax and send a video of one of your competitions. Give as much information about the competition as possible, such as where, when and whom were you competing against.

If you are competing in a non-team sport such as golf, tennis, track, or swimming you can have yourself videotaped while demonstrating your swing, style, stroke, etc. Coaches in these sports are interested in seeing the mechanics of your skill while they can read about what you've accomplished versus other athletes.

Video Tips· Be sure to send information about what team color and what number you are.· Be sure to label the video with your information- (name, jersey color and number, and phone number)· Don't expect to get these videos back- in fact don't even ask for them back.· Wait to send the video until the coach requests it. Coaches won't even view the video until they are confident you are a qualified recruit.· Provide only enough tape for your video: don't send a video with two hours of tape. Very often they will give a discount for large volume orders. When providing a game tape, make sure the competition is strong. Keep the entire playing field in view. Avoid focusing the camera just on you.· Show your mistakes as well as your great plays.· Edit out as much dead time as possible.· Show segments from two separate competitions if possible.

Note**If you don't feel comfortable or still unsure of how to make that all important video. Consult a professional video sports highlight professional.
If you need a more structured format for your resume, follow the sample form below:

General Data
Name:
Address Home Phone Number:
Date of Birth:
Place of Birth:
Number of Family Members:
Your contact information: Phone - Email

Mother's Name - Mother's Phone - Email
Father's Name - Father's Phone -Email

Academic
Name of High School/Junior College
Address City State Zip Graduation Date
Name of High School Counselor -Phone Number for Counselor
Current GPA Class Rank
PSAT Date Verbal Score Math Score Combined:
SAT I Date Verbal Score Math Score Combined:
SAT II Date Verbal Score Math Score Combined:
ACT Date Score :
General Athletic Data:
Name of Program Address of Program:
Name of Coach Coach's Phone: Email
Best Time to Call Height Weight Number of Years Played Titles
Held:
Leadership Positions:
Weight Training Program:
Note: Be sure to send game schedule.
In addition to the general athletic information given above, provide
athletic data specific to your sport. The two forms below for
basketball and football will give you the idea.

Athletic Data Basketball
Position:
Shots Attempted Shots Made %:
Free Throws Attempted Free Throws Made %:
Assists Steals:
Defensive Rebounds:
Offensive Rebounds:
Vertical Jump (express in inches):

Athletic Data Football
Check & Provide Pertinent Information
Offensive Positions
1) Quarterback Throws Right & Left Completion %
# of Touchdowns Thrown
2) Running Back Yards Gained On Ground Total Yards

Of Touchdowns # Of Passes Caught
Of Yards Gained
3) Tight End # Of Touchdowns
4) Wide Receiver Passes Thrown Passes Caught
Of Touch Downs
Defensive Position
Of Tackles # Of Interceptions
Of Sacks Touchdowns Total Yards Throwing
Of Carries Yards Gained Touchdowns
Of Receptions Yards Gained Touchdowns Punts Attempted Punts
Made Field Goals Attempted Field Goals Made
Kickoffs In End Zone
Reached 10 yd. Line
Reached 20 yd. Line
Strength—Bench Press Squat Clean
Speed – 40 yd. Time
You may also choose to use a professional service to write and
develop your resume. If you can afford it and want to go this route,
there is certainly nothing wrong with hiring it done. There are many
quality resources that focus strictly on writing creative, professional
and eye-catching resume.

FAQ
How many packets should I send out? We suggest 50-60. It is better
to have too many offers than not enough offers. Remember to send
them to different divisions NCAA Division I, II, III, NAIA and
NJCAA

How should I send this information? You can email the information
or send it via U.S. mail. Buy 9"x12" envelopes and put all of the
information neatly inside. You can also put information on both
sides of the paper to reduce costs. Avoid folding it up and mailing it
in a small envelop.

When should I hear something? You should hear something in 1-2
weeks or as long as 1-2 months depending upon the time of year you
sent the information and what the coach has going on. Be patient,
that means don't start calling the coach 2 days after you mailed it.
But, also be persistent and after a couple of weeks, call and follow-

up with the coaches to see if they have received the packet and have any questions.

<u>What if I don't have videotape?</u> Think back to which parents videotaped the games. Ask to get a copy of one of their tapes. Also, if you are reading this in advance of your senior year, you can plan to get someone to video you while you are competing.

Chapter 8
Are you a Senior in High School? - Don't Panic Just Yet

Whether you are a senior who has neglected doing any of the things necessary to gain exposure to college coaches or you're a senior who has done everything right and has simply fallen through the cracks, either way you may still yet have a good chance for an athletic scholarship provided you have the appropriate GPA and SAT/ACT scores.

Make sure that you have registered with the NCAA Initial Eligibility Clearinghouse, taken all the right classes, and have acceptable scores on the SAT/ACT tests.

Many athletes knock themselves out of contention simply because they fail to meet the academic requirements for admission. They mistakenly think that the academic issues will be overlooked if they can run the 40-yd dash in 4.3 seconds.

Though the scholarship opportunities are dwindling fast, there will still be programs that have scholarships left. Here's why; coaches tend to save some scholarships hoping and waiting for those super recruits who actually end up signing with other schools.

These prospective recruits have indicated verbally that they are committed to signing but at the last minute some of them simply change their minds and actually sign on the dotted line with another school.

Additionally, some coaches just haven't located the talent they need yet. Both of these scenarios are good news for you no matter which category you are in. If you are a senior who is a late starter, get aggressive and very aggressive right now. You have zero time to lose. Make a list of at least twenty schools that offer your sport where you would be interested in attending and playing.

Call the coaches on your list and let them know that you are interested in their programs. Tell them that you think your talents might benefit their programs. Ask them what you need to do to be considered for their programs.

You can also E-mail, send introductory letters, and resume marketing packets as outlined in the previous chapter. Use any method you can to get yourself into their recruiting systems: do it now! do not wait any longer.

Contact people who already know you. Talk with your high school coach, athletic director or any other individual in the community who might have contacts with college coaches or who might have played sports at the collegiate level. Ask them to assist you in your campaign to get an athletic scholarship. This is not the time to be shy. You will very often be pleasantly surprised by what people will do for you when you ASK. Typically, most Division I schools know one year ahead of time who they will be recruiting for a particular year.

Therefore, generally speaking, you will have better luck locating and securing a scholarship at this late date at a Division II, Division III, NAIA, or NJCCA school.
Some of these schools offer many of the same benefits that the Division I schools offer. The end result will be the same: you will receive a college education.

If you are a senior who has followed all the advice in this guide and you still haven't landed a scholarship, now is also the time for you to look at other options.

First, you'll need to re-adjust the focus of your recruiting campaign. Now is the time to broaden your search to include the Division II, Division III, NAIA, and NJCCA schools.
Keep in mind as you search that there are still many coaches all over the country that are still looking for eligible talented people to fit their programs.

These coaches are under as much pressure to find good recruits, as you are to find the scholarship. There are more than 1700 colleges and universities in this country with athletic programs, and you've contacted only a very small percentage of them.

Stay optimistic and don't give up. Just make a new list, which includes a couple of schools where you're sure to get in and start the whole process over.

First ---- Make another list of 50 -60 schools where you would be interested in attending and playing. Place phone calls to the coaches at the top 10- 20 schools.

Second---- Send introductory letters to the coaches at all 50 -60 schools. Send the letters even if you've already called the coaches.

Third----Wait for 1-2 weeks to hear from the coaches, then call and follow-up on the letter you sent.

Fourth----Fill out and return all questionnaires sent to you. Return them with a resume packet and, if requested, a video.

Last---To keep yourself in the minds of the coaches that have shown any interest in you, send monthly updates of newspaper clippings, athletic and academic achievements, and awards.

Other Options: Since you are starting so late, you will probably have to be a little more flexible and also think of other avenues to reach your goals.
For example, a Division I school wants you, but cannot give you a scholarship for the upcoming year, would you still want to go to that particular school enough to secure a government grant or pay your own way for that first year?

Would you consider being a walk-on the first year and hope for a scholarship the second year? Or, would you rather go to a smaller Division II school and receive an athletic scholarship immediately?

The walk-on does not receive an athletic scholarship. If your goal is to play college level athletics at a powerhouse school, this is certainly the more difficult and challenging road to take, however, it is one way that many, many athletes have chosen to start their college athletic careers and many of them have gone on to become star athletes.

Without question, walk-ons have to work harder to prove themselves. All walk-ons are given the chance to show the coach what they can do.

Also, a walk-on usually practices with the team, receives first choice of classes, and preferred housing. When considering the walk-on option, ask the coach about future scholarship opportunities provided you prove that you're team material. Division III schools do not offer athletic scholarships, however, the coaches at these schools often know of handsome academic scholarships and grants you might be eligible for.

These schools are usually smaller, private schools with an environment totally different from the large university schools. Some of you might be happier attending and playing in this type of setting. Another viable option is the JUCO (Junior College) route. Consider playing for a community college the first year or two. Some of these schools do offer athletic scholarships.

Click on http://www.njcaa.org/for athletic scholarship information. If not, tuition can usually be paid for with government grants. Some of the grants cover everything including room, tuition, and books. Additionally, many JUCO's offer work opportunities. Junior colleges do not deserve the negative perception that many people have about them. They are not the last ditch chance for dummy's to get into college.
In reality, they are basically a place to get your first two years of college, earn an associate degree, or get a 2-year certificate.

They also offer an opportunity for you to participate in your sport at an elite level. Use this link to search for junior colleges: If your dream is to play at the Division I level, the JUCO option provides a setting for you to improve academically and athletically.
Some four-year athletic programs can see your potential but they want you to have time to grow an inch or two, gain more strength, or possibly they want to see a more advanced level of maturity.

For a variety of reasons, they may want you, but they want you a year from now when you've had time to mature physically and emotionally and when you've had more time to refine your athletic skills. The Division I schools often use the JUCO athletic programs much like the major leagues use their farm teams. As with the four-year program, you will need to be proactive in your search for an athletic scholarship at a JUCO. They too do not have the budgets to recruit extensively and will welcome your introductory phone calls and materials.

If you are talented enough to play at the Division I or II level but need a little seasoning, you will more than likely be real asset to a JUCO program. If you've already passed the college entrance exam, you will be eligible to transfer to a four-year college and receive an athletic scholarship the next year. Finally, if you've reached your senior year in high school without securing an athletic scholarship, you may want to consider hiring a listing, recruiting or scouting service.

Many are reputable, quick, and effective. Since time is of the essence at this point, using one of these services may be the answer to your problem. They already have on file the names and addresses of all the college head coaches and they have the staffing and expertise to quickly prepare professional, detailed resumes.

Some of them may also have valuable contacts at many colleges and universities and may even know a coach who is looking for your particular talent. These services will take your unique information, prepare your marketing package, and have the package delivered to every coach you designate. At this late date, you're in a bind and this strategy will save a lot of time and energy and will also greatly reduce your stress level.

Again, do your homework on these services and make sure they can deliver what they promise. Talk with other people who have successfully used the service. Don't be afraid to ask for references.

Chapter 9
NCAA, NAIA, NJCAA

Colleges and universities with intercollegiate athletic programs are governed by one of three organizations: the National Collegiate Athletic Association (NCAA), the National Association of Intercollegiate Athletics (NAIA) and the National Junior College Athletic Association (NJCAA).

These associations establish uniform rules for the sports they govern, run championships and establish eligibility requirements for student athletes.
You will need to know which association governs the college(s) you're considering and what rules apply to you to ensure that you are eligible.

What does NCAA mean? The National Collegiate Athletic Association (NCAA) is the oldest and largest national sports organization in the United States, and its job is to set guidelines so that everyone plays by the same set of rules.

The NCAA represents thousands of college athletic programs and operates three divisions, Division I, II and III. So, what are the differences between the three divisions? This chapter contains a lot of technical data, and it will answer most of your basic questions.

You, more than likely, are not going to be anxious to read this stuff, but it will be advantageous for you to familiarize yourself with the rules governing the NCAA organization at the school where you are being recruited.
Know this information for yourself; don't depend on anyone else to interpret it for you. If you are in doubt about any rule as it might apply to you, contact the NCAA at:

The National Collegiate Athletic Association
P.O. Box 6222
Indianapolis, Indiana 46206-6222
317-917-6222 (phone)

317-917-6622 (fax)
NCAA Hotline: 800-638-3731
NCAA Eligibility Center 877-262-1492
http://www.ncaa.org/

Sadly, some coaches, when anxious to recruit you, may not always adhere to the governing rules of the NCAA. The vast majority of coaches and their recruiting staff are honest; however, the few who are not could lead you into an ineligible situation. Make it your business to know the NCAA recruiting rules as they may apply to you. Ignorance of these rules could cost you your scholarship.

NCAA- Division I (326 schools) There are 120 Division I A schools. These schools represent the highest level of competition and the Division I A schools offer the most scholarships. They, as a general rule, have the highest caliber of athletes; and also have larger student populations.
Division I also has 1A and 2A Football. Typically, a student/athlete is required to focus on his or her sport year-around.

A Division I institution must sponsor a minimum of either seven sports for men and seven sports for women or six sports for men and eight sports for women with two team sports for each gender. Each playing season has to be represented by each gender as well.

An institution may award athletic scholarships to student-athletes and the number of scholarships an institution may award varies from sport to sport. Division I schools must meet minimum financial aid awards for their athletics program, and there are maximum financial aid awards for each sport that a Division I school cannot exceed. Football is the only sport where the NCAA splits its top division into Division I-A and I-AA. Division I-AA has 206 colleges that offer full and partial scholarships. Programs must meet minimum attendance requirements to attain the I-A designation.
Academic Eligibility Requirements: Check with the www.ncaa.org for the latest requirements.

To be eligible to participate in Division I or Division II athletics, students must register and be certified by the NCAA Initial-

Eligibility Center, your counselor, coach or athletic director can obtain registration materials, at no cost by calling the Eligibility Center at 877-262-1492 or you may also register on their website at http://web1.ncaa.org/ECWR2/NCAA_EMS/NCAA.html.

In order to be registered with the NCAA eligibility center, you must complete the student-release form and mail or fax the top (white) copy of the form to the eligibility center along with the $$$$$ registration fee. High school counselors may waive the eligibility center fees if you have previously qualified for and received a waiver of the ACT or SAT fee. Fee-waiver information is specified on the student-release form. Give the yellow and pink copies of the form to a high-school official who then sends the yellow copy, along with an official copy of your high-school transcript, to the eligibility center. Your counselor should keep the pink copy on file at the school. When your high school closes for the summer, your school must send the eligibility center a copy of your final transcript that confirms graduation from high school.

By completing the form, you authorize your high school(s), to release academic information (such as transcripts and test scores) to the Eligibility Center. If you have attended more than one high school (grades 9-12), you will list those schools to release your transcript to the eligibility center. You do not need to contact previous schools or send them copies of the student release form; the eligibility center will contact the school(s) to get the information they need.

NCAA-Division II (279 schools)
Division II schools are smaller and are sometimes specialty schools. They provide scholarships, as well as financial aid and grants. Division II teams usually feature a number of local or in-state athletes. Many Division II student-athletes pay for school through a combination of scholarship money, grants, student loans and employment earnings. Division II schools do compete with some Division I schools.

Division II schools must sponsor a minimum or four sports for men and women, with two team sports for each gender. An institution may award athletic scholarships to student-athletes, and the number of scholarships an institution may award varies from sport to sport. There are maximum financial aid awards for each sport that a Division II must not exceed.

The Division II schools also require that you be a high school graduate and have a minimum GPA and SAT/ACT scores. Student/athletes must register and be certified by the NCAA Eligibility Center. Your counselors can obtain registration materials, at no cost, by calling the eligibility center at 877-262-1492 or you may also register on their website at ncaa.com.

In order to be registered with the eligibility center, you must complete the student-release form and mail or fax the top (white) copy of the form to the eligibility center along with the $$$$$ registration fee. High school counselors may waive the eligibility center fees if you have previously qualified for and received a waiver of the ACT or SAT fee. Fee-waiver information is specified on the student-release form. Give the yellow and pink copies of the form to a high-school official who then sends the yellow copy, along with an official copy of your high-school transcript, to the eligibility center. After your high school closes for the summer, your school must also send the eligibility center a copy of your final transcript that confirms graduation from high school

ELIGIBILITY: NCAA FRESHMAN ELIGIBILITY REQUIREMENTS Division II

*Achieve a specified minimum SAT score and or ACT score;
NCAA- Division III (420 schools)
Most Division III schools are smaller private schools that place a high priority on academic strengths and pride themselves on their prestigious academic reputations. Therefore, the cost is typically substantially higher than for the Division I and Division II Schools. Often, athletes are recruited only after they have established themselves as serious students.
The obvious benefit to a Division III school is the opportunity to receive an education from one of the top academic schools in the

nation while also having the opportunity to continue your athletic career.

Division III schools have to sponsor at least five sports for men and five for women, with two team sports for each gender, and each playing season represented by each gender.

Division III athletics departments place special importance on the impact of athletics on the student-athletes rather than the spectators. The athletic participant's experience is of paramount concern. These schools encourage participation by maximizing the number and variety of athletic opportunities available to students, placing primary emphasis on regional in-season and conference competition.

Division III schools cannot provide athletic scholarships, but can provide academic scholarships, financial aid, grants and work-study programs. These institutions are not allowed to award any type of financial aid based in any way on athletic ability.
If you plan to attend a Division III college, you may receive financial aid up to the cost of attendance (tuition and fees, room and board, books, transportation, and other expenses incidental to attendance) if the aid is based on financial need and is not associated with athletic ability.

ELIGIBILITY: NCAA FRESHMAN ELIGIBILITY REQUIREMENTS DIVISION III

Eligibility, financial aid, practices and competition is governed by institutional, conference and other NCAA regulations. However, the NCAA does not establish eligibility requirements for student athletes in Division III schools.

**There are waivers of the initial-eligibility requirements that may be granted based on evidence that demonstrates circumstances in which your overall academic record warrants a waiver. The school that is recruiting you must initiate the request for the waiver.
**The rules for minimum GPA, SAT/ACT, etc are applicable for athletic eligibility. Your admission to a school is governed by the entrance requirements of that particular school.

FAQ

What are the major differences between Division I, II and III?
Typically, as you move up from Division III to Division I etc.; you
will find bigger, stronger, faster and more accomplished athletes. A
few pounds and inches are usually added with each position. In
general the more talented players are found at the higher levels;
however, this is not written in stone and many professional athletes
have come from smaller schools.

What if I am home schooled, how do I qualify? All prospective
student-athletes who are home-schooled will need to have their core-
course requirements analyzed by the NCAA Committee on Initial-
Eligibility Waivers. The best thing to do is contact the NCAA
membership services for information regarding home schooling.

*How can I make sure that I'm not doing something to make me
ineligible to play?* If you are unsure about anything contact the
NCAA, NAIA or NJCAA immediately and they will be happy to
answer your questions.

*I currently compete in two sports in high school and would like to
continue playing both sports in college, is this possible?* Yes,
Division III schools actually have many athletes who are competing
in three sports. There are some Division I and Division II schools
that have dual-sport athletes. However, it is tougher to compete in
two sports at these levels because the demand on your time is more
at these levels.

How many years can I receive an athletic scholarship? Student-
athletes are allowed up to five years of scholarships, awarded one
year at a time.

What is a player-agent and can I use one? The player-agent markets
your athletic ability and represents you in contract negotiations or in
commercial endorsements. If you are a blue-chip player and one of
these individuals contacts you, it should raise a RED FLAG. They
see great potential in your athletic abilities and are trying to get their
foot in the door early on. They will not represent themselves as

agents, but as someone interested in your overall welfare. Please be careful in any meetings you might have with player-agents. If you have concerns about a player-agent, contact your high-school coach, director of athletics or the NCAA national office for assistance. NCAA rules don't prohibit meetings or discussions with an agent. However, you jeopardize your college eligibility in a sport if you agree (orally or in writing) to be represented by an agent while in high school or college, regardless of whether the agreement becomes effective immediately or after your last season of college eligibility. Also, receiving any benefits or gifts by your family or friends from a player-agent would jeopardize your college eligibility.

NAIA (300+ schools) The National Association of Intercollegiate Athletics (NAIA) membership is comprised of approximately 300 fully accredited four-year colleges and universities throughout the United States and Canada.

The NAIA governs championships in the following sports: baseball, basketball cross-country, football, golf, soccer, softball, swimming and diving. Tennis, track and field (indoor and outdoor), and volleyball. The NAIA has divisions (I and II) for men and women's basketball, but for all other sports, the schools are classified together.

There are many advantages to competing in NAIA sports. Besides the benefit of close-knit communities and small class sizes on the typical NAIA campus, NAIA offers:· Maximum opportunity to participate in regular season contests and National Championships;

*Flexibility to transfer without missing a season of eligibility.
*Fewer recruiting restrictions.
*Focus on the education and character development of the student-athlete.

The NAIA recruitment process is less cumbersome, with fewer restrictions on the contact a student-athlete and coach can make. More frequent communications aids in assuring that the student-athlete is comfortable with the choice of institution. In the event the student-athlete feels that the school or team is not the right fit, he/she can transfer to another NAIA institution and compete the next season without sitting out a year. While NAIA rules hold strict academic requirements, the process of establishing eligibility is streamlined since there is no eligibility center.

For a copy of the NAIA Guide for College Bound Student, call: 918-494-88 http://www.naia.org/local/collegebound.html can find out about colleges that belong to the NAIA by clicking on http://www.naia.org/index.html
NAIA ELIGIBILITY REGULATIONS: Click for more detailed http://www.naia.org/local/collegebound.html regulations.

FAQ
NAIA Questions

What is the length of my scholarship and what type of scholarship is it? Most institutional scholarships are for only one year. Also, there are some scholarships that cover just tuition (or housing, or books) and others that cover housing, books, tuition, or full-ride scholarships.

Is there financial aid available for summer school? Some athletes prefer to simply take the necessary course hours to be eligible to play during the season. This could leave you with several credit hours that you may wish to pick up during the summer. However, you may need financial assistance in the summer, so ask whether or not your financial aid packages cover summer expenses.

If I get seriously injured and I am unable to participate, what will happen to my scholarship? Institutions are not obligated to offer scholarships or financial aid past the terms of the agreement. It is important to know what the institution's commitment to injured athletes is.

May I be employed while receiving a scholarship? Find out if you can be employed while in season, or out of season. Also, find out if you can be employed during vacations without violating your scholarship.

What is a typical day for a student-athlete? You will learn a typical schedule that will include courses, practices, meal times, study times, etc. This will give you insight as to how to manage your time and assist you with needed adjustments.

What percentage of athletes graduates in four years? This will tell you about a coach's commitment to academics. Also, the team grade point average is a good indicator of academic commitment.

Would my major mix well with athletics? Some majors are more time consuming than others and may require labs or mandatory work outside of class hours. You need to know the demands that will be placed on you within your major, to know if you are spreading yourself too thin by participating in athletics.

Is my degree respected from your institution? There are some institutions that have stronger programs than others. There are also those institutions that specialize in specific degree programs.

What role will I play on your team? Many coaches will already have an idea of how they would like to utilize certain recruits. You will be able to find out where the coach sees you fitting in on his/her team and why.

What demands does this sport require physically and what time is required? It is important to know the physical demands that will be placed on you during your tenure as an athlete. Also, you need to know how much time is spent with this sport so you may manage your study time wisely.

What is your coaching style? All coaches have different coaching styles and use different techniques for motivation and discipline. It is to your benefit to ask this question to determine whether your learning style and the coach's style would be a good fit.

NJCAA (510 schools)
The National Junior College Athletic Association (NJCAA) represents over 500 schools that are two-year colleges and are divided into three divisions with scholarships offered only at the Division I and II levels.

Division I colleges may offer full scholarships, and Division II colleges are limited to awarding tuition, fees and books. Division III institutions may provide no athletically related financial assistance. However, NJCAA colleges that do not offer athletic aid may choose to participate at the Division I or II level if they so desire.

The NJCAA sponsors championships in a variety of sports: fall and spring baseball, basketball, bowling, cross country, football, fall and spring golf, ice hockey, spring and fall lacrosse, marathon, track and field (indoor and outdoor), fall and spring softball (fast pitch), fall and spring soccer, swimming, fall and spring tennis, fall and spring volleyball, and wrestling.

Tuition for junior college is typically much less than for four-year schools. Generally, the class sizes are smaller and if you are not quite ready for a four-year university; this is a wonderful way to get prepared. Recently, some junior college football programs have gotten together and staged an NFL-style combine for four-year coaches to evaluate talent coming out of junior colleges. For information on the NJCAA write: NJCAA, P.O. Box 7305 Colorado Springs, CO 80933-7305 Or go to the NJCAA web site: www.njcaa.org

ENTRY REQUIREMENTS
Grade Point Average: High school graduate or pass GED Minimum SAT/ACT Scores: Check with admission for each school

Whose rules do I abide by? Students participating on an intercollegiate level in any one of the certified sports of the NJCAA shall conform to the requirements of the Rules of Eligibility, the rules and regulations of the conference with which the college is affiliated, and also the rules of the college at which the students are attending.

How do I determine my initial eligibility? Due to the unique academic and athletic situation of each individual, and the complexity of the NJCAA eligibility rules, it is recommended that each potential student-athlete discuss their eligibility with the athletic personnel at the NJCAA college they have chosen to attend. Should the athletic staff have any questions in determining an individual's eligibility, the college may contact the NJCAA National Office for assistance.

Must I have graduated from high school? Students must be a high school graduate or must have received a high school equivalency diploma or have been certified as having passed a national test such as the General Education Development Test (GED).

How many seasons may I participate in a sport? Students are allowed two (2) seasons of competition in any sport at a NJCAA college, if they have not participated at any intercollegiate level during two (2) seasons previously. Playing in one or more regularly scheduled contests prior to post-season competition uses one season of participation in that sport.

What about All-Star competitions? The NJCAA National office must approve student participation in athletic events such as All-Star games. The NJCAA does NOT restrict the number of All-Star games in which a High School student may participate prior to attendance at a NJCAA college.

Must I be a full-time student during the season? Students must maintain full-time status during the season of the sport (s) in which they have chosen to participate (full-time status being 12 credit hours or more).
For more information concerning the NJCAA-www.njcaa.org

Chapter 10 -
College Athletic Scholarship - Putting It All Together

When is a student considered a prospective student/athlete? Once a student begins the ninth grade even if they are currently not participating in sports.

Technically, what does "recruited" mean? When a coach or other college representative approaches a prospective student/athlete or a family member of a prospective student/athlete about playing sports at a specific college.

When can a college coach legally contact a student/athlete? The student/athlete may at anytime contact a coach, but prior to the high school junior year, college coaches can send or have sent only a general informational packet about the school.
Beginning in the junior year, college coaches can send recruiting materials about their programs and schools.

While college coaches are prevented from sending recruiting materials or approaching a student/athlete before the beginning of the junior year, student/athletes may contact a coach by any means available.

For example, if you were to send a letter of introduction to the coach during your sophomore year, the coach would probably put your letter in his possible recruit file and would probably begin to keep his eye on you. He or she will have three years to watch you. To keep your file up-to-date, send the coach evidence of your successes such as newspaper clippings, awards received, tournaments won and the like. The more coach exposure you gain, the better your chances for a scholarship.

How many campus visits can a recruit make on his or her own? A recruit can make as many visits to a campus as they like at their own expense.

Therefore, a big advantage to in-state universities is that a prospect can easily visit and see if the school is something they would like to check into further.

How many "official visits" can a recruit make? During a recruit's senior year, they can make five "official visits" to colleges, with a limit of one per particular college.
These limits apply even if a recruit plays more than one sport. Before the recruit can visit, the college must have received the recruits high school transcript and ACT/SAT scores.

How many times can a coach visit the recruit or a recruit visit the campus? The NCAA allows college coaches to have seven recruiting opportunities per prospect during the academic year.
These opportunities fall into two categories: The face-to-face meeting and the off-campus activity used to assess a recruits academic qualifications or athletic ability.

What does the NCAA consider a face-to-face meeting? The NCAA defines contact as "any face-to face-meeting between a college coach and recruit or a recruits parents in which you say more than hello." Contact also is defined as a meeting that has been pre-arranged or occurs at a recruit's high school or a competition, regardless of what is said. No more than three of the seven recruiting opportunities may be in person, off-campus contacts.

What does the NCAA consider an evaluation? The NCAA defines evaluation as "any off-campus activity used to assess a recruits academic qualifications or athletic ability."
That would include watching practice or competition at a recruit's school, at a camp or combine or any other site---even if "contact" doesn't occur.

How long is the recruit allowed to visit on campus? The NCAA says the visit must not exceed 48 hours. The college can pay for the visit. The recruit can receive round-trip transportation, and the recruit and their parents can receive meals, lodging and tickets in the general seating area--not special areas-for athletic events. Complimentary souvenirs paid for by the university are not allowed, (that means t-shirts, shorts, key chains, hats, etc…)

What are the rules for printed materials given out by a coach to a recruit? Beginning on September 1st, a school may give to you an official publication and videotape of the school; general correspondence with attachments that must be printed with black ink; a media guide or recruiting brochure.
An athletic game program and a student-athlete handbook can be given with official visits.

Can I tryout for a Division I sport? Absolutely not!!

What are the rules regarding a coach contacting a recruit? There can be no off-campus contact allowed before July 1st of a recruit's junior year. No more than three off-campus contacts are allowed for all sports, except football, which allows seven.

When can a college coach call? With the exception of football, the following telephone rules apply.
No calls are allowed from booster club members or alumni--**EVER.**
No calls are allowed from faculty members and coaches until July 1st after the student's junior year.
After July 1st, a coach or faculty member may call one time per week (to you, parents, or guardians).

More frequent calls may occur during five days leading to an official campus visit, on the day of a coach's off-campus contact with a recruit or on the first three days of signing the National Letter of Intent.
**For Division I-A football, a coach may call a recruit once during May of your junior year and then may not call again until September 1st of your senior year.
**For Division II-A football, coaches may telephone a recruit once during the month of May of their junior year in high school and then not again until September 1st of their senior year in high school.
Also, football coaches can telephone a recruit as often as they wish during the period 48 hours before and 48 hours after 7 a.m. on the

initial signing date of the National Letter of Intent. Outside of the contact period, a football coach may only call you once a week.

When can a college coach, faculty members write a prospective recruit? Letters from coaches, faculty members aren't permitted until September 1st at the beginning of a recruit's junior year.

When can alumni and boosters contact a recruit? Never!!! Not in any way--letters, phone calls, are prohibited with the exception of the regular admissions process that applies to all students.

Can I compete in all-star Games? After you have completed your high-school eligibility and before you graduate, you are allowed to participate in two high-school all-star football or basketball contests in each sport. Most often AAU competitions do not count as All-star games-but be sure to check.

Can I transfer? If you are transferring from a four-year or two-year college to a NCAA school, you must satisfy certain requirements before being eligible to participate in athletics at that institution.

Can a player-agent contact me and represent me in contract negotiations? NCAA rules don't prohibit meetings or discussions with an agent.

However, you jeopardize your college eligibility in a sport if you agree (orally or in writing) to be represented by an agent while in high school or college, regardless of whether the agreement becomes effective immediately or after your last season of college eligibility. Also, receiving any benefits or gifts by you, your family or friends or a player-agent would jeopardize your college eligibility.

Can I accept sweatshirts, t-shirts, shoes, cash, cars or any gifts from coaches? A recruit can't accept any gift from anyone associated with any university. By accepting any gift, the recruit could make himself or herself ineligible.

Contact period: permissible for authorized athletic department staff members to make-in-person, off-campus recruiting contacts and evaluations during specific times during the year. You can view these calendars for the different sports at the www.ncaa.org

Dead period: Not permissible to make in-person recruiting contacts or evaluations on or off campus or permit official or unofficial visits.

Evaluation Period: Permissible for authorized athletics department staff to be involved in off-campus activities to assess academic qualifications and playing abilities. No in-person, off-campus-recruiting contacts with a prospect are permitted.

Quiet Period: Permissible to make in-person recruiting contacts only on the member institution's campus.
Athletic Tryouts: A Division I or III member institution on its campus or elsewhere is not permitted to conduct (or have conducted on its behalf) any physical activity (e.g. practice session or test/tryout) at which one or more prospects reveal, demonstrate or display their athletics abilities in any sport.

A Division II institution member institution may conduct a tryout of a prospect only on its campus or at a site at which it normally conducts practice or competition and only under the following conditions:
1. No more than one tryout per prospect per institution is permitted.
2. The tryout may be conducted only for high-school seniors who are enrolled in a term other than the term in which the traditional season in the sport occurs or who have completed high-school eligibility in the sport and written permission has been obtained from the high school's athletics director; for a two-year college student, after the conclusion of the sport season, and for a four-year college student, after the conclusion of the sport season, provided written permission to contact the prospect has been obtained.
3. A medical examination of a prospect conducted by an institution's regular team physician or other designated physician shall be permitted as a part of the tryout.
4. The tryout may include tests to evaluate the prospect's strength, speed, agility, and sport skills. Except in the sports of football, ice hockey, lacrosse, soccer and wrestling, the tryout may include

competition. In the sport of football, the prospects shall not wear helmet or pads.

5. Competition against the member institution's team is permissible, provided such competition occurs during the academic year and is considered a countable athletically related activity.

6. The time of the tryout activities (other than the physical examination) is limited to the length of the institution's normal practice period in the sport, but in no event can it be longer than two hours; and during the period of tryout.

7. The institution may provide equipment and clothing on an issuance-and-retrieval basis to a prospect during the period of a tryout.

NAIA Rules: The NAIA has a complete set of rules at its website at www.naia.org

NJCAA Rules

What are the rules for an official visit at a junior college? A school may pay for an athlete to visit the campus for no more than two days and nights. The visit must be completed no less than 10 days prior to the opening date of classes. The school can pay for the student meals with spending limits equal to the amount college employees may spend for meals while traveling on college business. A school may not entice an athlete to attend with gifts.

Does the NJCAA allow tryout? Yes with certain restrictions.

Where can I find out more about specific rules of the NJCAA? The website at: http://www.njcaa.org/

How many letters can a coach send to a recruit? One coach reportedly sent nine hundred recruiting letters to a single athlete to show how committed the school was to that athlete.

What is the NJCAA Letter of Intent? The NJCAA Letter of Intent is used to commit an individual to a specific institution for a period of one year. The form is only valid for NJCAA member colleges and has no jurisdiction over NCAA or NAIA colleges.

What is the NJCAA Scholarship Certification? he NJCAA Scholarship Certification is designed to inform the student/athlete, in writing, how much athletic aid is being provided by the institution.

This form binds the school to the student for the amount of aid specified on the form.

What if I signed a NJCAA and a NCAA Letter of Intent? A student is allowed to sign a Letter of Intent with both a NJCAA and a NCAA college without sanction. The student may not, however, sign a NJCAA Letter of Intent with two NJCAA colleges. If a student does sign with two NJCAA colleges, that student will become immediately ineligible to compete in NJCAA competition for the next academic year in any sport.

One NJCAA school can offer me a full scholarship, and one school can't offer me anything. Why? Each institution belonging to the NJCAA can chose to compete on the Division I, II, or III level in designated sports.

Division I colleges may offer full athletic scholarships.

Division II colleges are limited to awarding tuition, fees and books, and Division III institutions may provide no athletically related financial assistance.

However, NJCAA colleges that do not offer athletic aid may choose to participate at the Division I or II if they so desire.

I am a recent high school graduate and coaches have started to recruit me to play. What is allowed?
1. No institution shall permit an athlete to be solicited to attend by the promise of a gift or inducement other than an athletic grant-in-aid.
2. An institution may pay for one visit to its campus by direct route, for a stay not to exceed two days and two nights. The visit must be completed no less than 10 days prior to the opening day of classes.
3. While recruiting a potential athlete on campus, a college representative may purchase meals for the athlete. The value of the meals may not exceed the amount provided to a college employee while traveling on college business.
4. A college official must authorize all funds utilized for recruitment purposes.

For further clarification of the recruiting rules, see Article VIII, B. If a student-athlete signs a NJCAA Letter of Intent, all NJCAA institutions are obligated to respect that signing and shall cease to recruit that student-athlete. The student-athlete is obligated to notify any recruiter who contacts him/her of the signing.

NOTE: Although every attempt has been made to make sure that the above rules and regulations are accurate, YOU should check directly with the member organizations to make sure that you are completely up-to-date with any rule concerning your recruiting program. We have provided direct links to all three organizations in this chapter.

Thank You

If you have gained some helpful information from this book, I would really appreciate an honest review on Amazon. The information in this book has worked for countless others and it can work for you too.

Be sure to visit our website at CollegeAthleticScholarship.com and sign up for our newsletter and receive additional information on getting a college athletic scholarship.

Wishing you all the best,

Athletic Scholarship Info

CPSIA information can be obtained
at www.ICGtesting.com
Printed in the USA
LVOW03s0345290917

550506LV00019B/756/P